THEODORE ROOSEVELT, THE U.S. NAVY, AND THE SPANISH-AMERICAN WAR

The Franklin and Eleanor Roosevelt Institute Series on Diplomatic and Economic History

General Editors: Arthur M. Schlesinger, Jr., William J. vanden Heuvel, and Douglas Brinkley

FDR AND HIS CONTEMPORARIES
FOREIGN PERCEPTIONS OF
AN AMERICAN PRESIDENT
Edited by Cornelis A. van Minnen
and John F. Sears

NATO: THE FOUNDING
OF THE ATLANTIC ALLIANCE
AND THE INTEGRATION
OF EUROPE
Edited by Francis H. Heller
and John R. Gillingham

AMERICA UNBOUND
WORLD WAR II AND THE MAKING
OF A SUPERPOWER
Edited by Warren F. Kimball

THE ORIGINS OF U.S. NUCLEAR
STRATEGY, 1945–1953
Samuel R. Williamson, Jr. and
Steven L. Rearden

AMERICAN DIPLOMATS IN
THE NETHERLANDS, 1815–50
Cornelis A. van Minnen

EISENHOWER, KENNEDY, AND
THE UNITED STATES OF EUROPE
Pascaline Winand

ALLIES AT WAR
THE SOVIET, AMERICAN,
AND BRITISH EXPERIENCE,
1939–1945
Edited by David Reynolds,
Warren F. Kimball, and A. O. Chubarian

THE ATLANTIC CHARTER
Edited by Douglas Brinkley and
David R. Facey-Crowther

PEARL HARBOR REVISITED
Edited by Robert W. Love, Jr.

FDR AND THE HOLOCAUST
Edited by Verne W. Newton

THE UNITED STATES AND THE
INTEGRATION OF EUROPE
LEGACIES OF THE POSTWAR ERA
Edited by Francis H. Heller and
John R. Gillingham

ADENAUER AND KENNEDY
A STUDY IN GERMAN-AMERICAN RELATIONS
Frank A. Mayer

THEODORE ROOSEVELT AND
THE BRITISH EMPIRE
A STUDY IN PRESIDENTIAL STATECRAFT
William N. Tilchin

TARIFFS, TRADE AND EUROPEAN
INTEGRATION, 1947–1957
FROM STUDY GROUP TO COMMON MARKET
Wendy Asbeek Brusse

SUMNER WELLES
FDR'S GLOBAL STRATEGIST
A Biography by Benjamin Welles

THE NEW DEAL AND PUBLIC POLICY
Edited by Byron W. Daynes, William D.
Pederson, and Michael P. Riccards

WORLD WAR II IN EUROPE
Edited by Charles F. Brower

FDR AND THE U.S. NAVY
Edward J. Marolda

THE SECOND QUEBEC
CONFERENCE REVISITED
Edited by David B. Woolner

THEODORE ROOSEVELT,
THE U.S. NAVY, AND THE
SPANISH-AMERICAN WAR
Edited by Edward J. Marolda

THEODORE ROOSEVELT, THE U.S. NAVY, AND THE SPANISH-AMERICAN WAR

EDITED BY
EDWARD J. MAROLDA

palgrave

First published 2001 by PALGRAVE™
175 Fifth Avenue, New York, N.Y.10010 and
Houndmills, Basingstoke, Hampshire RG21 6XS.
Companies and representatives throughout the world

PALGRAVE is the new global publishing imprint of St. Martin's Press LLC Scholarly and Reference Division and Palgrave Publishers Ltd (formerly Macmillan Press Ltd).

ISBN 0–312–24023–6

Library of Congress Cataloging-in-Publication Data
Theodore Roosevelt, the U.S. Navy, and the Spanish-American War / edited by Edward J. Marolda.
        p. cm.
Papers originally presented at a symposium held at the U.S. Navy Memorial's Heritage
Center, Washington, D.C., Oct. 21, 1998.
    Includes bibliographical references and index.
    ISBN 0–312–24023–6 (hc)
    1. Spanish-American War, 1898—Naval operations—Congresses. 2. United States. Navy—History—Spanish-American War, 1898—Congresses. 3. Roosevelt, Theodore, 1858–1919—Career in the Navy—Congresses. 4. Spanish-American War, 1898—Influence—Congresses. I. Marolda, Edward J.

E727.T47   2001
973.8'9—dc21

                                                              2001032757

A catalogue record for this book is available from the British Library.

Design by Letra Libre, Inc.

First edition: October 2001
10 9 8 7 6 5 4 3 2 1

Printed in the United States of America.

Contents

PREFACE

THE SPANISH-AMERICAN WAR OF 1898 WAS A TURNING POINT in the development of the United States Navy. For at least a decade before the conflict, forward-thinking American political leaders and naval officers had pressed for the creation of a fleet of modern, steel-hulled warships armed with the most powerful weapons. Chief among these advocates for a "new Navy" were Theodore Roosevelt, an accomplished naval historian and Assistant Secretary of the Navy; and Captain Alfred Thayer Mahan, persuasive champion at the Naval War College of a strategic theory whose central concept called for command of the sea by an oceangoing fleet of battleships.

The swift and overwhelming U.S. victory in the war validated the views advanced by Roosevelt, Mahan, and other proponents of naval expansion. The American navy, despite problems coordinating all of its operations with the U.S. Army and hitting enemy ships with its gunfire, handily destroyed the Spanish naval squadrons at the battles of Manila Bay and Santiago de Cuba. The Spanish government understood that loss of sea control had doomed its insular empire and promptly sued for peace. Almost overnight, the United States acquired control of Spain's overseas possessions in the Caribbean and the Western Pacific.

The war also had a marked institutional impact on the Department of the Navy in the early years of the twentieth century. Mahan, Stephen B. Luce, Henry C. Taylor, William S. Sims, and other reformist officers pressed successfully for improved management, administration, and logistical support of the Navy and for professionalization of the officer corps. American sailors enjoyed the adulation of the public for their martial performance in the war. Ironically, life in the service for most enlisted men changed little as a result of the victory. Rigid discipline, racial and ethnic discrimination, and the rigors of shipboard life hurt reenlistments and sent desertion rates soaring. The experience of the Spanish-American War provided the U.S. Marine Corps, searching for an expanded mission at the turn of the century, with powerful ammunition. The hard-fought defense of the anchorage at Guantánamo by

Lieutenant Colonel Robert Huntington's 1st Marine Battalion won the admiration of many Americans and provided an example of how similar Marine units could protect the fleet's advance bases in the newly won overseas empire of the United States.

The Spanish-American War was a defining event not only in the evolution of the Navy and Marine Corps but in the life of Theodore Roosevelt. The future commander in chief burnished his considerable political and intellectual skills with a demonstration of leadership and bravery under fire at San Juan Hill and El Caney. This personal experience and the strategic success achieved by the Navy exerted powerful influences on President Roosevelt's subsequent "big stick" foreign policy. Moreover, Theodore Roosevelt's enthusiasm for the Navy and the sea lived long after him in the extended Roosevelt family, and especially in his illustrious cousin Franklin Delano Roosevelt.

Victory over the Empire of Spain in this short, sharp conflict marked America's debut on the world stage. An energetic, self-confident, and determined generation of Americans then considered it their duty to spread the blessings of democracy, Christianity, and unbridled capitalism to the world and carve out a place for the United States alongside the great powers of the globe. President Theodore Roosevelt was the driving force behind that ethos, and the U.S. Navy was its symbol.

In commemoration of the Spanish-American War of 1898, on October 21, 1998, the Theodore Roosevelt Association, the U.S. Navy Memorial Foundation, and the Naval Historical Center sponsored a symposium entitled "Theodore Roosevelt, the U.S. Navy, and the Spanish-American War." The daylong event was held in the U.S. Navy Memorial's Naval Heritage Center in Washington, D.C. A highlight of the event was an inspiring address by The Honorable John H. Dalton, Secretary of the Navy. Participating in the conference were the Spanish Ambassador to the United States, The Honorable H. E. Antonio de Oyarzabal, and military attachés of the Spanish Embassy. Throughout the day, scholars distinguished by their broad understanding of Theodore Roosevelt, his dynamic impact on the development of the U.S. Navy, and the 1898 war between the United States and Spain presented new interpretations of their subjects. Professor H. W. Brands, author of *T. R.: The Last Romantic,* presented an insightful luncheon address. A reception hosted by the sponsoring organizations concluded the memorable symposium.

Special thanks are due Lawrence H. Budner, President, Theodore Roosevelt Association; Rear Admiral Henry C. McKinney, USN (Ret.), President, U.S. Navy Memorial Foundation; and Dr. William S. Dudley, Director of Naval History, for their gracious sponsorship of this symposium. Also deserving of thanks is Professor Douglas Brinkley of the Eisenhower

Center at the University of New Orleans, who reviewed these proceedings; Dr. Maria Zehren of the U.S. Navy Memorial, who helped coordinate the event; and Ms. Debbie Gershenowitz of Palgrave, who used her considerable editorial skills to place this scholarly work before you.

Edward J. Marolda

ONE

THEODORE ROOSEVELT, THE NAVY, AND THE WAR WITH SPAIN

ANNA K. NELSON

ABOUT 50 YEARS AGO, A VERY POPULAR PLAY, *Arsenic and Old Lace,* began its long run in American high schools. It was about two elderly ladies who poisoned their elderly gentlemen callers with elderberry wine. Periodically, a clearly manic young man who thought he was Theodore Roosevelt would come on stage with round glasses and mustache, dressed in pith helmet and shorts or army cavalry uniform. He would shout at the top of his lungs, "Charge!," and leap up the stairs, presumably up San Juan Hill. In spite of the repetition, the line was always good for a laugh.

While this character bore little resemblance to the former president, it does indicate something about public knowledge of Roosevelt's accomplishments. It is ironic that Theodore Roosevelt is so often depicted in an army uniform as the commander of the "Rough Riders" on the landmass of Cuba. Roosevelt was a Navy man. His army career was brief, to say the least, and his real contribution to the Spanish-Cuban-American War went far beyond his celebrated career with the Rough Riders.

Even as a young boy, Teddy Roosevelt was enamored with the Navy. Ships and adventures on the high seas intrigued him. He defied convention by pursuing this interest, and his senior thesis at Harvard, *The Naval War of 1812,* was published in 1882, eight years before Alfred Thayer Mahan published *The Influence of Sea Power Upon History.*

When the election of 1896 ensured Republican control of both the legislative and executive branches of government, Roosevelt wanted nothing more than to be assistant secretary of the Navy. When his friends, including Senator Henry Cabot Lodge of Massachusetts, approached the newly elected William McKinley, they found him concerned about Roosevelt's bellicose reputation. McKinley explained to them that he wanted a peaceful presidency and feared that Roosevelt's conduct would lead to war.

Finally persuaded that Roosevelt would be a loyal supporter of his administration, McKinley made the appointment. It was a greater opportunity for influence than even Roosevelt had foreseen. His superior, Secretary of the Navy John D. Long, was a man of little energy, who preferred long vacations in New England to working and had lengthy visits with the doctor who took care of the painful corns on his feet. Roosevelt, on the other hand, was a man of prodigious energy who learned more about the inner workings of the U.S. Navy in one week than Long would learn throughout his entire term of office.

Roosevelt set out to build up the Navy and cultivate the powerful people who could influence the passage of large appropriations. Mahan became his collaborator. The officer supplied arguments for Roosevelt, and the latter tried to further Mahan's views by publicizing his articles. Although Alfred Thayer Mahan influenced Roosevelt's views, he was only one of a larger group of influential associates. Before Roosevelt came to office in 1897, he had already aligned himself with a coterie of men, including Henry Cabot Lodge, Brooks Adams, and John Hay, who were devoted to a "larger policy," the overseas expansion of American interests. These men were both intellectually involved in seeking a new American paradigm and politically involved in solving the issues of the day.

Roosevelt and Lodge, for example, were disappointed that Hawaii had yet to be annexed, and exerted their influence to convince McKinley to overcome that deficiency even before the war with Spain. They chafed over public indifference to foreign affairs at a time when all the great powers were carving out empires while the Americans were being left behind. They believed in the superiority of the Anglo-Saxons and took to themselves the responsibility for taking care of "lesser" peoples.

But Roosevelt and his fellow expansionists, unlike their twentieth-century successors, were not concerned with promoting American economic interests. Their primary concern was national power and prestige. "I wish to see the United States the dominant power on the Pacific Ocean," Roosevelt wrote. "Our people are neither craven nor weaklings and we face the future high of heart and confident of soul eager to do the great work of a great power."[1] Consistent with their forbears, they turned to the tradition of "Manifest Destiny" to differentiate their plans for world power from those of the European imperialists.[2]

Observing the success of Great Britain, the growth of Germany, and the increasing dominance of Japan as a Pacific power, the expansionists looked for a common denominator. It was easily found. Strong, imperial powers had large, world-class navies. For the United States to take its proper place in the world, it must also have a great navy. Roosevelt's public explanation was that a large navy would prevent war. He wrote that if the United States built and maintained an "adequate" navy and made it clear that "we are perfectly ready and willing to fight for our rights, then the chances of war will become infinitesimal."

But there was a second purpose in Roosevelt's mind. In Howard Beale's words, Roosevelt believed that "the Navy was an instrument of national policies that could not be carried out without it." Roosevelt saw the Navy as a protector, a strategic necessity for an active, great power. He wanted a large navy so that the country could "take the position to which it is entitled among the nations of the earth."[3]

As Assistant Secretary of the Navy, Roosevelt set out to build this impressive navy; a navy strong enough to fight a war, and important enough to make the United States into a world power. McKinley's views notwithstanding, Roosevelt also had a war plan for his navy a year before the war with Spain actually began. His plan would entail a naval blockade of Cuba that would lead to the liberation of Cuba, not its annexation. If necessary, because of the war, the Navy would attack the Philippines. Again the United States would not plan to annex the Philippines, but rather have a "controlling voice." Thus, while Roosevelt's navy was making the United States safe for peace, it was busy preparing for war, a war President McKinley was not eager to declare.

The ink was barely dry on the declaration of war when Roosevelt the adventurer ordered his uniform from Brooks Brothers and went off to fight against Spain. He acquitted himself splendidly and never forgot the hours he spent on San Juan Hill. Nevertheless, his few months as a cavalryman were of little consequence compared to the impact of a message he sent to the commander of the Asiatic Squadron, Commodore George Dewey. Judging that war would come sooner rather than later, Roosevelt sent Dewey a message that allowed him to move swiftly into Manila Bay once war was declared. Dewey prepared his ships, took on coal, and, when the United States was finally at war, destroyed the Spanish squadron in the Philippines. This move alone was a lasting contribution, for better or for worse, of Roosevelt as Assistant Secretary of the Navy.

In many ways, Roosevelt and the war of 1898 had a kind of symbiotic relationship. The war itself was a result of the efforts of Roosevelt, Lodge, Mahan, and others to send a message to the world, especially Great Britain, that "America is now a great power. Ignore it at your peril." On the other hand, it is doubtful that Roosevelt could have accomplished his goals if there had been no war with Spain. Tensions were growing, the Hearst papers were all but screaming about Spanish brutality, the expansionists were pushing McKinley, and the Cuban "exiles" were not-so-secretly abusing the neutrality acts. Critical of McKinley's unwillingness to declare war to assuage the ills of the Cubans, Roosevelt was convinced that war would ultimately come and that the United States had to be prepared.

The coming war allowed Roosevelt to put the Navy in "good shape." He was able to get the appropriations from Congress and faced no interference from McKinley. Roosevelt firmly believed that the United States must have a great navy to take its place in the world. The war gave Roosevelt the ability to begin building that navy, which, in turn, helped turn the country into a Pacific power.[4]

After a term as Governor of New York, Roosevelt was nominated to be vice president in the election of 1900. In a matter of months, McKinley was dead from an assassin's bullet and Theodore Roosevelt was President of the United States, an accidental president who entered office with strong views concerning the future of the country.

Roosevelt, heir to the heritage of Polk and Seward, always regarded the United States as a Pacific power as well as an Atlantic power. He was impressed by the rapid modernization of Japan and its success in the Sino-Japanese War of 1895. Roosevelt saw Japan as a potential threat to American interests in the Far East (East Asia); hence his message to Dewey and the annexation of the Philippines. Of course the annexation of Hawaii provided the United States with sovereignty over islands far from the nation's shores. But as a mere glance at a map will illustrate, annexing the Philippines moved U.S. strategic interests into the heart of Asia. It was partly to ensure the presence of U.S. interests in the Pacific that Roosevelt sent American battleships around the world, perhaps the best known of his efforts at naval foreign policy. The "Great White Fleet" was impressive, especially when it sailed into Japanese harbors. The Japanese were so impressed they stepped up the building of their own navy.

As president, Roosevelt turned more and more of his attention to Japan. His Nobel Peace Prize came as a result of his role in the Treaty of Portsmouth, which marked the conclusion of the Russo-Japanese War. His mediating hand moved to equalize power between these two nations, but Roosevelt made no move to create a large American presence in either Japan or China. He was nothing if not realistic about the limitations of American power or the Navy's ability to compete with the great powers that had already divided up China.

Instead, he turned his attention to his neighbors. Hegemony, after all, usually begins in the "neighborhood." Since the war cleared the Caribbean of foreign spheres, this area was the natural spot for the United States to express its newly discovered power. Groups of islands and coastal cities lent themselves to the foreign policy of a big navy. Roosevelt tackled instability through intervention and economic control, and he tackled the problem of concentrating a two-ocean navy by building the Panama Canal. The problem of passage over the isthmus and the first attempts to move a squadron from one ocean to another had beviled the United States since its founding years. The war with Spain exacerbated that problem, as each squadron was bound to its ocean. Enemies would not wait for ships to make the lengthy trip around the hemisphere. The effort begun before the Civil War to build a canal across the continent suddenly became a priority for President Roosevelt. The machinations involved in his effort to gain consent for an isthmian canal across Panama certainly did not constitute Roosevelt's finest hour, but the need for a canal was entirely consistent with Roosevelt's worldview of national power based upon a strong, battleship navy.

Many historians argue that the war with Spain in 1898 was the true beginning of the twentieth century. Under the leadership of Theodore Roosevelt, the first twentieth-century president, it marked the emergence of the United States as a global power. Influenced by conversations with old friends and mentors, by his experience as Assistant Secretary of the Navy, and by the causes and effects of the war with Spain, he came to office unusually well equipped for the presidency.

Roosevelt's expansionism was tied to his belief in the United States as a world power. An important component of this drive to world power was his use of the Navy to express—some would say flaunt—the power of America. He was remarkably consistent in his worldview and was clever in the use of his office to promote that view. For a president who never had to fight a war (hot or cold), he left an impressive foreign policy legacy.

On September 9, 1998, the *Washington Post* ran an advertisement sponsored by the Newport News Shipbuilding Company. The ad featured a bird's-eye view of an impressive aircraft carrier, its planes on deck in orderly rows. Above the picture of the carrier was the message: "90,000 tons of Diplomacy"[5]: Roosevelt would have approved.

NOTES

1. Howard Beale, *Theodore Roosevelt and the Rise of America to World Power* (Baltimore: Johns Hopkins University Press, 1984), 50.
2. For a discussion of the views of Lodge and Roosevelt, see chap. 3 of William C. Widenor, *Henry Cabot Lodge and the Search for an American Foreign Policy* (Berkeley: University of California Press, 1980).
3. Beale, *Theodore Roosevelt*, 50–51.
4. Kenneth Wimmel, *Theodore Roosevelt and the Great White Fleet: American Sea Power Comes of Age* (New York: Brasseys, 1998), 85–114.
5. *Washington Post*, Sep 9, 1998, 4.

NEW INTERPRETATIONS OF HOW THE USS *MAINE* WAS LOST

DANA WEGNER

THE U.S. BATTLESHIP *MAINE* EXPLODED IN HAVANA HARBOR at 9:40 P.M. on February 15, 1898. Within six days of the explosion a U.S. naval court of inquiry was convened to establish the cause of the explosion. One month later the court found that the ship, in all probability, was destroyed by an underwater mine that ignited parts of the forward magazines. The act had been done by unknown persons. Relations between the United States and Spain were tense during a period of Cuban colonial rebellion and Spanish repression. On April 25, 1898, the United States declared war on Spain and "Remember the *Maine*" became a familiar call to arms. Between 1910 and 1912 the wreck of the *Maine* was raised from Havana Harbor and the Navy briefly reexamined the case, essentially rubber-stamping the 1898 findings.

ADMIRAL RICKOVER AND DESTRUCTION OF THE *MAINE*

On September 1, 1974, the *Washington Star-News* published an article by John M. Taylor entitled "Returning to the Riddle of the Explosion that Sunk the *Maine.*" The riddle was whether a Spanish or Cuban mine planted outside the ship, or some cause within the ship had initiated the explosion. Admiral Hyman G. Rickover (1900–1986), powerful head of the U.S. Navy's nuclear propulsion program, read the Taylor article with accelerating interest.

It stated that the Navy had made little use of its technically trained officers during its investigation of the tragedy. For example, George W. Melville, the Navy's Chief Engineer, was among those who strongly doubted that a mine was the agent of destruction, but he was never asked for his views. According to the article, doubts still persisted about the official versions of the disaster. The admiral could not believe that the Navy had not made use of all available information to determine the cause.

Rickover read the article on Sunday; early Monday morning he was in the historian's office of the Energy Research and Development Agency, brandishing the newspaper. At that time I was a historical researcher on Admiral Rickover's staff reporting to Dr. Francis Duncan, an Atomic Energy Commission historian. Our assignment was to prepare a study of the naval nuclear propulsion program. Because we were naval historians, Rickover wanted to know what we knew about the investigation of the *Maine.* When we replied that we did not know any details, he asked us to see what we could find out. Our own curiosity aroused, we agreed to do so. The admiral was intrigued. If the Spanish-American War marked a decisive point in American history, why was there so little detailed knowledge about the event that precipitated the conflict: the destruction of the *Maine?*

But going further into the question of the *Maine* meant delving into the raw material of history: government records, contemporary newspapers and periodicals, documents stored in archives, collections of personal papers, artifacts in museums, and perhaps even interviews with descendants of people involved in the catastrophe. Because of his official duties, he could not undertake research into such source materials. He asked if we would do so.

Dr. Duncan and I talked and corresponded with relatives of *Maine* survivors and victims, questioned diplomatic and admiralty law historians, and examined many collections of private and public papers dealing with the loss and the salvage of the ship. At the National Archives it was clear that we were not covering new historical ground. Nevertheless, bound by Admiral Rickover's insistence on thoroughness, we dutifully had all the material brought out for us to review.

I was particularly intrigued by one six-inch-thick binder of documents. It was a file of reports sent from Havana to the Navy's Bureau of Construction from 1910 until 1911 by William Ferguson, the U.S. naval constructor assigned to help the Army recover the wreck. In 1910, President Taft had assigned the Army Corps of Engineers the task of raising the *Maine* from the slime and mud in which she had rested for 13 years. The next year the engineers built a cofferdam around the site and slowly pumped out the water. The complete unwatering of the wreck still stands as one of greatest engineering achievements of the Army.

Some people might have thought that raising the hulk and then ceremoniously sinking it in deep water in 1912 had destroyed the evidence. Ferguson's weekly reports contained photographic prints of the tedious step-by-step process of unwatering the ship. However, when the site was uncovered, photographs showed the mangled wreckage of the ship exposed to the air and essentially unmoved since the disaster in early 1898. As shown in the pictures, constructor Ferguson had clearly identified exact elements of the ship's structure in the wreckage by painting frame and strake numbers directly upon the twisted plating. Ferguson's report was not newly uncovered at the archives. Any number of historians had seen it before and probably overlooked it as relating only to the recovery of the wreck and being "too technical" to be important.

I believed that Ferguson's reports and photographs, coupled with the numerous builder's plans of the ship, might provide enough information for modern engineers to offer an opinion about the cause of the explosion. With great trepidation, we brought the proposal to the admiral. Challenged and intrigued, he soon realized that there was a book in the making.

THE HANSEN-PRICE ANALYSIS

Recognizing that what he needed were experts both in explosives and their effects upon ship hulls, Rickover phoned the commanding officers of the Navy's David Taylor Model Basin and the weapons center at White Oak, Maryland. Without explaining, he said he wanted two of their best people at Crystal City the next day. The admiral obtained the services of Ib S. Hansen, then Assistant for Design Applications in the Structures Department at the David Taylor Naval Research and Development Center (David Taylor Model Basin) at Carderock, Maryland, and Robert S. Price, a research physicist at the Naval Surface Weapons Center at White Oak. Leaders in their field, both men had decades of experience in analyzing the effects of explosions on ship hulls.

After receiving a degree in engineering, Ib Hansen had seen action as a young member of a structural demolition team serving with the Danish resistance during World War II. He emigrated to the United States as a bridge designer and in 1960 became a researcher for the U.S. Navy at the David Taylor Model Basin. A true pioneer in the field of structural dynamics and the effects of weapons against ships, Hansen had directed firsthand and had analyzed nearly a thousand live explosive tests against ships. Also a trained engineer, Robert Price had worked for the Navy in the field of underwater explosions since 1943. He had been commissioned to study the loss of several ships and had also conducted and studied many explosive tests. I cannot imagine anyone in the United States, perhaps in the world, better qualified to investigate the *Maine*.

Rickover made available to Hansen and Price a room in which they could spread out their materials, told us to give them any support they needed, and left them alone. Apart from a first meeting and a final one convened to present their completed report, the admiral had no contact with either man during the formulation of their study.

At the first meeting with Ib Hansen and Bob Price, we laid out copies of the photographs of the wreckage. Hansen and Price, who had never met before, shuffled through the pictures and plans and within a surprisingly short time generally concluded that the explosion that had killed 266 American sailors in 1898 had originated inside of the ship. To their experienced eyes, the center of the explosion was clearly identifiable and the skin of the ship showed no plausible evidence of penetration from the outside.

Hansen and Price retreated and began drafting their technical report. The scholarly report not only would reveal their straightforward observations about the center of the explosion, but would also take into consideration conflicting eyewitness accounts and the errors of the Navy investigations in 1898 and 1911. Unlike the earlier investigations, Hansen and Price were careful to explain their lines of thought and offer supporting documentation.

While Hansen and Price wrote their analysis, by mid-1975 we started to draft the historical section of the book. We needed to explain how the ship came to be in Havana Harbor on that fateful night and how the Navy conducted its inquiries into the loss. Frequently, we sent manuscript into the admiral's office. From his penciled comments it was evident that he had read and pondered every word, at times striking paragraphs and substituting his own to make sure the text said exactly what he wanted it to say.

All of us recognized the importance of Ib Hansen and Bob Price's report. After covering all of the significant aspects of the case in their text, Hansen and Price concluded that the locus of the explosion was on the port side at frame 27—an area corresponding to the ship's six-inch reserve magazine. The total weight of ammunition in the forward part of the ship was more than 72,000 pounds. 10,000 to 20,000 pounds of propellant gunpowder had exploded, including most of the 11,000 pounds in the reserve magazine and the partial contents of several surrounding larger magazines. Hansen and Price found no evidence of characteristic tearing and mangling of the outside skin in the explosion area, and they concluded that the source of the explosion was solely on the interior of the vessel. All of the wreckage now could be identified as having been created by the explosion of ammunition and the dynamic actions of the sinking of the ship. The two men were positive that the explosion originated fully within. The event that initiated the explosion, of course, could not be determined with as much certainty.

Hansen and Price speculated that, most likely, spontaneous combustion of coal in a bunker adjacent to the reserve magazine caused a common bulkhead between the two compartments to overheat and ignite improperly stowed ammunition. Coal bunker fires were well known and potentially catastrophic, but little advertised within the U.S. Navy. Warships at that time were designed with coal bunkers surrounding their magazines and boilers.

American warships had been designed with common bulkheads between the bunkers and magazines because the preferred fuel was smokeless anthracite coal, and anthracite coal was not subject to spontaneous combustion. After many steel ships had joined the fleet, however, the Navy switched to more volatile bituminous coal. While it burned hotter and the ships steamed faster, it was also subject to self-ignition and the Navy was, at least until the ships could be refitted, stuck with common bulkheads between many bunkers and magazines. A number of bunker fires had been reported aboard American warships at the time the *Maine* blew up, and several cases nearly caused their loss. A heat transfer study conducted in 1997 concluded that, given the circumstances postulated by Hansen and Price, a coal bunker fire could have caused the *Maine*'s ammunition to explode.

THE 1898 COURT OF INQUIRY

In the summer of 1897, the United States warned Madrid that the war in Cuba must end. In October 1897, the *Maine* was at Port Royal, South Carolina, ready to be sent to Havana if called. In December 1897, Spain was again warned and the *Maine* advanced to Key West. On January 23, 1898, the North Atlantic Squadron arrived off Key West and, after being joined by the *Maine* and other vessels, proceeded to the anchorage at the Dry Tortugas. The next day the *Maine* was deployed to Havana. She arrived with short notice and anchored under the pretext of a friendly visit, but remained at a high state of combat readiness. The presence of the *Maine* in Havana and the resumption of friendly visits was not a sign that tensions between the United States and Spain were easing. They were increasing. The so-called friendly visit was a small but calculated show of force and posture. One has only to ponder the coincidence of the American ship's exploding while in Havana at a time when emotions on both sides were already running high.

The loss of the *Maine* had to be investigated, but we found that the investigation could have been done differently. The Secretary of the Navy could have personally chosen the members of the court of inquiry, but instead he decided to rely upon routine procedures. He assigned the task to the commander in chief of the North Atlantic Squadron, who oddly proposed a list of relatively junior line officers. The fact that initially the officer chosen to be court president was junior to the commanding officer of the *Maine* would indicate either ignorance of Navy regulations or that, in the beginning, the court did not intend to examine the possibility that the ship was lost by accident and the negligence of her captain. Captain William Sampson was eventually chosen as president, and he was senior to Captain Charles D. Sigsbee of the *Maine.*

With the inquiry held mainly afloat in Havana Harbor, the Navy Department in Washington answered as best it could requests from the court for the ship's plans and for an advisory naval constructor. Nevertheless, from the membership of the court to the competency of its few expert witnesses, we found that the investigation lacked the "blue ribbon" quality we are accustomed to today, even for less important matters. Admiral Rickover believed that the investigation was below par, even for its day.

The 1898 Navy court of inquiry presented its results in two parts. The proceedings consisted mainly of transcripts of testimony. The findings were the facts as determined by the court. There was a broad gap between the proceedings and the findings. The court left no record of the reasoning that carried it from the often-inconsistent witnesses to the conclusion that an external explosion had destroyed the ship.

The major piece of physical evidence, the court concluded, was a portion of the *Maine's* keel. It could be seen by the naked eye protruding well above the surface of Havana Harbor. A thin ligament still connected the intact and upright aft two-thirds of the ship with her twisted bow, now mostly submerged and lying on its side. How could the keel be displaced from the bottom of the ship and end up above the main deck level? The court asserted that only an underwater mine could have done it.

Curiously, the court had brought in only one technical witness, Commander George Converse, who had been in charge of the Torpedo Station at Newport, Rhode Island. Under questioning, the president of the court read to Converse a hypothetical sequence of physical events in which a coal bunker fire ignited the contents of the six-inch reserve magazine and the wreckage of the ship was created by the resultant explosion and dynamic actions of the vessel sinking. With unusual clarity, what we now know to have happened was introduced in court. The president asked Commander Converse if he believed that the described sequence could have occurred. Converse simply stated without elaboration that he could not realize such an event happening.

The court's verdict of an external explosion was one that could be expected. The strained relations between the two nations, the warlike and patriotic atmosphere in Congress and the press, and the natural tendency to look for reasons for the loss that did not reflect badly upon the Navy might have been predisposing factors in the court's findings. Had the ship blown up in an American or friendly foreign port, and had the same type of damage occurred, it is doubtful that an inquiry would have laid the blame on a mine. The findings of the court of 1898 appear to have been guided less by technical consideration and more by the awareness that war was now in-evitable. Indeed, war preparations were under way before the Navy court's findings were officially announced.

Spanish authorities in Havana extended every courtesy to the survivors of the *Maine*. They provided medical attention and a place to bury the dead. They guarded the wreck from the curious press and even performed their own investigation on the spot. Though they were not given access to wreck by the U.S. Navy, their commendable inquiry was, in several ways, more perceptive than the American version. They found that the ship most likely exploded by accident. Needless to say, the United States gave the Spanish investigation scant notice.

THE 1911 BOARD

The U.S. Navy board of 1911 could do its work free from the risk of war. Moreover, several of its members were engineers and better qualified for their task than were the line officers of 1898. In 1911 they could examine the wreck under the best possible circumstances. The board's report, ordered printed by Congress on December 14, 1911, was difficult to understand, partly because its exhibits were not printed and partly because, like the 1898 inquiry, the reasoning behind its conclusion was not given.

The 1911 board based its finding—that a mine destroyed the *Maine*—on a discovery in the area of the wreck inaccessible to the 1898 court. After some mud was removed, it was found that the bottom of the ship had been damaged between frames 28 and 31 about 45 feet abaft the location of the explosion as divined by the 1898 inquiry. One section of plating was bent inward and folded back with one edge remaining attached to the outer bottom. The exposed edge of an adjacent plate was also bent inward slightly. The 1911 board stated that a mine caused this damage, but not the upthrust keel so important to the 1898 investigators.

It is difficult to understand why the board took this position. The displacement of the bottom plating could have been accounted for by an internal explosion and the dynamic effects of the ship's sinking. More important, the displaced plating did not exhibit the scars that would be expected from a mine explosion. The 1911 board depended upon naval constructor Ferguson's photographs and models, the proceedings and findings of the 1898 court, and visits to the wreck. So far as the records show, the 1911 board, like the 1898 court, carried out its investigation without the advice of any outside experts and without the help of available technical information.

Perhaps, but this is only speculation, the 1911 board was willing on technical grounds to overturn the fundamental conclusion of the 1898 court regarding the upthrust ship's keel, though unwilling to raise the question

whether there had been a mine at all. Only 13 years had elapsed since the
nation had gone to war with the battle cry "Remember the *Maine*." It would
have been difficult for the board to raise the issue whether the nation and its
constituted authorities had made a grave error in 1898.

CONTEMPORARY ANALYSES

Not everyone agreed then nor agrees now that the riddle of the *Maine* has
been answered once and for all. Some critics believe that Admiral Rickover's book, *How the Battleship Maine Was Destroyed*, has not made the case
of an internal explosion and that somehow the Hansen-Price analysis is in-
conclusive. However, no serious consideration of the controversy is possible without taking the book into account. Today, after a quarter of a
century of studying the loss of the *Maine*, Ib Hansen and Robert Price
have not altered their conclusions. They believe that critics of their report
are those who do not understand the document or the discipline. A few
academic historians are fond of claiming that, like most events long ago
documented by the written word, the cause of the *Maine's* loss never can
be truly known; however, these historians have not understood the valid-
ity of applying modern engineering expertise to the study of the technical
record. That record includes technical reports, measurements, descriptions, and photographs created during the recovery of the wreck of the
Maine in 1910–1911.

Events surrounding the 1998 centenary of the loss of the ship encouraged the public release and donation to the U.S. Naval Academy Museum
of a letter held by the family of Lieutenant John J. Blandin, USN, an officer and survivor (later victim) of the *Maine*. Writing to his wife the day
after the tragedy, Blandin explained: "No one can tell what caused the explosion. I don't believe the Spanish had anything to do with it. . . . Don't
publish this letter."

During the centenary year, in addition to many television shows, there
appeared several new books and articles in the United States and Spain that
purported to challenge the Hansen-Price findings. The Rickover team was
disappointed that some of these productions and publications, especially a
feature article in *National Geographic* magazine, apparently were motivated
commercially, dramatically, and journalistically to portray a continuing
"mystery" surrounding the loss of the ship when, in fact, the question had
been fully answered by Admiral Rickover in 1976.

The *National Geographic* article was particularly disturbing, since it probably was read by millions of people around the world. The editors employed
a marine engineering firm to restudy the event using computer analyses. The

mere application of omniscient computers bestowed an undeserved veracity upon the seriously flawed resultant report. Computer programs applied to the problem were ill-suited for the task, and the results were further skewed by input of incorrect data concerning the structure of the ship and manner of ammunition storage. The report correctly concluded that a coal bunker fire could have ignited the *Maine's* ammunition, and it erroneously concluded that a mine could have done the same. More enthralled with misguided computer calculations than reality, the author's of the report and the related *National Geographic* article did not adequately account for the fact that the photographs of the wreckage simply do not show any plausible evidence of mine damage.

The divergence of technical opinion in 1998 split largely between younger, inexperienced scientists who were highly reliant on elaborate computer models and older, seasoned engineers who compared photographs of the wreckage with their own firsthand experiences in the field. Accordingly, even the marine engineering firm secured by *National Geographic* was fractured by internal disagreement when a respected and experienced naval structural engineer, who was also an executive in the firm, sided with the Rickover group and rejected many of his own team's findings.

The Rickover team had not been informed about *National Geographic's* publication plans and the new investigation until the flawed study was substantially and intractably complete. Regardless of motivation, *National Geographic's* secretive early approach discouraged professional collaboration, thereby "muddying the water" and insuring that the magazine would reap the publicity benefits of contrasting "expert" opinions. Unable to resist temptation, much of the media in the United States and Spain unfortunately followed suit in 1998 and branded the loss of the ship still an unsolved mystery or an enigma.

One can only lament that *National Geographic* did not seek a collaborative effort among their editors, the Rickover team, and the contractor performing the new investigation. Instead of presenting the contrived "continuing mystery," *National Geographic* could have clarified the public's understanding of the causes of the loss of the *Maine* by offering a definitive answer to the question.

The Rickover team stands resolute, believing that contrary opinions are based upon poor historical research and/or bad engineering. Hopefully, the hoopla created by the media for profit and entertainment in 1998 will fade from the public's eye. There is no doubt that the Hansen-Price analysis has stood, and will continue to stand, the test of time. It is interesting to note that most nontechnical critics and admirers alike have focused on Hansen and Price's admitted speculation that spontaneous combustion of coal may have caused the magazines to ignite. Many people overlook the larger and more significant aspect of their findings, that is, with no doubt, that some internal event (whatever it might have been) caused the ship to explode. One of the major events to precipitate the Spanish-American War, therefore, was a tragic coincidence.

Admiral Rickover was convinced that the destruction of the *Maine* had important lessons to teach. Of these, the most important was the role of technology in making national decisions. Technical problems must be examined by technically qualified people who cast their analysis in terms other citizens can understand. Otherwise, fateful decisions will be made on the basis of emotions. The loss of the *Maine* reminds us that even small wars bring in their wake long-lasting, deep, and troubling entanglements.

REFERENCES

Allen, Thomas B. "Remember the Maine?" *National Geographic* 193, no. 2 (Feb 1998): 92–111.

———. "A Special Report: What Really Sank the Maine?" *Naval History* 12, no. 2 (Mar/Apr 1998): 30–39.

Arnot, Laurence A., comp. "USS *Maine* (1887–1898) in Contemporary Plans, Descriptions, and Photographs." *Nautical Research Journal* 36, no. 3 (Sep 1991): 131–47.

Blandin, John J. "Don't Publish This Letter." *Naval History* 12, no. 4 (Jul/Aug 1998): 30.

Blow, Michael. *A Ship to Remember* (New York: William Morrow, 1992).

Crawford, Michael J., Mark L. Hayes, and Michael D. Sessions. *The Spanish-American War: Historical Overview and Selected Bibliography* (Washington, D.C.: Naval Historical Center, 1998).

Hansen, Ib S. "In Contact." *Naval History* 12, no. 3 (May/Jun 1998): 8–16.

Hansen, Ib S. and Dana M. Wegner. "Centenary of the Destruction of the *Maine:* A Technical and Historical Review." *Naval Engineers Journal* 110, no. 2 (Mar 1998): 93–104.

Haydock, Michael D. "This Means War." *American History* 32, no. 1 (Feb 1998): 42–63.

Miller, Tom. "Remember the *Maine*," *Smithsonian* 28, no. 11 (Feb 1998): 24.

Price, Robert S. "Forum." *National Geographic* 193, no. 6 (Jun 1998): 30.

Remesal, Augustin. *El Enigma del* Maine (Barcelona: Plaza & Janes Editores, 1998).

Rickover, H. G. *How the Battleship* Maine *Was Destroyed* (Annapolis: Naval Institute Press, 1995). Includes new information not found in the original 1976 edition published by the Naval Historical Center. Also, *Como Fue Hundido El Alcorazado Maine* (Madrid: Editorial Naval, 1985). Spanish-language translation of the 1976 edition.

Smith, Roy C. III. "In Contact." *Naval History* 12, no. 4 (Jul/Aug 1998): 30.

Wegner, Dana. "In Contact." *Naval History.* 12, no. 4 (Jul/Aug 1998): 15–17.

————. "Raising *Maine* and the Last Farewell." *Nautical Research Journal.* 42, no. 4 (Dec 1997): 220–36.

————. Review of *Remembering the* Maine, by Peggy and Harold Samuels. *Naval Engineers Journal* 107, no. 5 (Nov 1995): 98–102.

This article reflects the views of the author and does not necessarily reflect the views of the Naval Surface Warfare Center or the Department of the Navy.

THREE

THE SPANISH NAVY AND THE SPANISH-AMERICAN WAR

REAR ADMIRAL MIGUEL A. FERNANDEZ, SPANISH NAVY

MORE THAN 450 YEARS AGO THE SPANISH CAME TO VIRGINIA and named the beautiful Bay of Chesapeake "Saint Mary's Bay." Spain gave the 13 American colonies enormous economic, logistical, and political support during the Revolutionary War, and as soon as peace consecrated the fruits of an allied victory, on October 27, 1795, the United States and Spain signed a treaty. The first article read: "There shall be solid and unbreakable peace and sincere friendship among his Catholic Majesty, his successors and subjects, and the U.S. and its citizens without exceptions as to persons or places." Notwithstanding the peaceful relations and the contribution of Spanish culture to the formation of the great American nation, something happened years later that led the two nations into an unwanted war. Why did these two former allies go to war? How did the Spanish Navy face this war?

Quoting President Woodrow Wilson some years later: "Is there any man in this room or any woman—let me say, is there any child—who does not know that the seed of war in the Modern world is industrial and commercial rivalry?"

POLITICAL SITUATION

The Monroe Doctrine determined U.S. foreign policy in the nineteenth century. It was based on territorial expansion as far away as Hawaii and the Philippines and on opposition to interference of the European powers in relation to the newly independent American nations. As Monroe said in his presidential message of December 2, 1823: "This will be considered dangerous to our peace and security." That still sounds familiar.

The United States always had its eye on Cuba, but it was mainly after the acceptance of "Manifest Destiny," a kind of mystic-political instrument, that the territorial expansion of the 13 colonies over the neighboring lands that belonged to the Spanish crown occurred. It must not be considered "imperialist expansion." On the contrary, it became an irresistible, divine impulse well beyond the control of the leaders in Washington. Alfred Thayer Mahan, a great strategist and naval publicist, always praised Cuba's commercial and strategic value, particularly in terms of its proximity to the Panama Canal. He insisted that it would be very easy for the United States to acquire Cuba, as well as Puerto Rico and the Philippines. Mahan, Senator Henry Cabot Lodge, and some others spread the expansionist idea in Congress and through publications like the *Atlantic Monthly*. They observed:

—Whether you like it or not, Americans shall look abroad.
—Hawaii and the future of our Naval Power are related.
—Naval Power is what makes a nation great.
—Cuba must be an American colony. If we cannot buy it, we shall get it by force.

Moreover, American business concerns were extremely interested in the island. Cuba provided many agricultural and luxury goods for the American dinner table, like rum, sugar, molasses, and tobacco. A different kind of business also mushroomed, something that always flourishes during an insurrection, weapons dealing and gun running. The Cuban rebels received most of their supplies through a rampant gun trade based in Florida. A New York City–based group of Cuban exiles and American sympathizers called "the Junta" was the brains behind this covert operation. They raised the money, bought the weapons, and arranged for their delivery. Spain, logically, became extremely suspicious of any American vessel that came within 20 miles of Cuba. This situation led to many incidents of Spanish naval vessels stopping U.S. merchant vessels on the high seas. The most significant incident was the seizure in 1873 of the *Virginius* steamer commanded by a U.S. Naval Academy graduate and well-known gunrunner named Joseph Fry. The Spanish steamer and sloop-of-war *Tornado* intercepted *Virginius*. Fry and 49 of his crew were tried and executed. An angry United States wanted to respond to this incident with force, but the U.S. Navy in those days was in no condition to wage that battle.

Later, taking advantage of the increasing Spanish political instability, the United States raised the level of confrontation. First, President Ulysses S.

Grant and then President William McKinley sent messages to Congress that when the inability of Spain to impose its authority and sovereignty over Cuba became obvious, the United States would do its duty.

The appointment in 1893 of General Valeriano Weyler as Governor of Cuba did not improve Spain's image in the United States. Weyler was the scapegoat and everybody blamed him for the suffering of the people. He enforced a harsh policy of reconcentrating peasants in certain sites in order to isolate the rebels. Interestingly, the United States used the same practice during the Civil War: reconcentration of peaceful citizens, embargoes, and property confiscation. Weyler's measures were no harsher than some used by the British in the Boer War or by the Americans themselves during the Philippine Insurrection and the Vietnam War.

However, despite pressure from the press, the public, and congressmen shouting "Cuba libre!" from the floor of the House of Representatives, U.S. presidents downplayed moves to intervene in Cuba. The White House wanted the fighting in Cuba to stop, but it did not want a war with Spain.

Over the years, there were several American attempts to buy the island of Cuba from Spain. An American Bank Syndicate was created to offer $100 million to Spain to abandon the island in 1897. Later on, President McKinley proposed to the queen regent to buy it for $300 million. Talks between the two nations began in the mid-1890s and lasted until the declaration of war in 1898. An historic truth prevailed: Spain did not want to sell. This was one of the reasons for the war. Yet Spain made important concessions to U.S. pressure. The queen regent reminded Ambassador Woodford that Spain had met all the promises made to the United States: replacement of General Weyler, home rule status for Cuba, and soft measures instituted by the new governor, Ramon Blanco y Arenas. She also suggested that President McKinley do something in return, like dissolving the New York "Junta."

The status of the insurrection in 1898 was very critical. It was close to being crushed by the Spanish Army when something unexpected happened, something that totally changed the political and military situation of Spain: the explosion of USS *Maine*.

THE EXPLOSION OF BATTLESHIP *MAINE*

Mr. Fitzhugh Lee, the American consul in Cuba at the time, expressed concerns about the safety of Americans living in Cuba and requested protection. This appears to have been a wrong conclusion because the riots, started by General Weyler's supporters, were by no means directed at Americans, but rather towards those who supported Cuban home rule. After many hesitations McKinley decided to send the battleship *Maine* to Havana.

Ordering the *Maine* to Havana did not mean that war was inevitable. Probably, the president was uncertain about what he should do. He would hardly have sent a battleship into Havana, with its narrow entrance guarded by strong fortifications, if he thought war was imminent. Nor would Spain have sent the *Vizcaya* to New York. Clearly, both governments tried to avoid war.

At 9:40 P.M. on February 15, 1898, the U.S. battleship *Maine* exploded in the harbor of Havana, Cuba. 266 officers and men lost their lives. The United States did not cooperate with the commission designated by Spain to investigate. The Spanish commission concluded that the explosion was a mere accident, probably due to a fire close to an ammunition magazine. In his 1976 book, *How the Battleship Maine Was Destroyed,* Admiral Hyman G. Rickover defended the same idea that there was no evidence that a mine destroyed the *Maine,* very much in line with the Spanish conclusion.

I was in the Naval Postgraduate School, Monterey, California, when Rickover's book was published, and I still remember how my fellow U.S. naval officers discussed the book privately, looking at me from the corner of their eyes. I told them: "You know now what we have known for years!" In Rickover's words: "The court's verdict of an external explosion was the only one that could be expected. The strained relations between the two nations, the warlike and patriotic atmosphere in Congress and the press, and the natural tendency to look for reasons for the loss that did not reflect upon the Navy, might have been predisposing factors in the courts findings."[1] And what about the board of 1911? Only 13 years had elapsed since the nation had gone to war with the battle cry "Remember the *Maine.*" It would have been difficult for the board to raise the issue of whether or not the nation and its constituted authorities had made a grave error in 1898.

All the efforts to avoid the war were fruitless. On April 11, President McKinley announced: "The United States has the right and the duty, in consideration to the principles of humankind and civilization and its own interest in compromise to demand and act to put an end to the war in Cuba." The resolution was adopted on April 18, 1898, almost unanimously in the House of Representatives and the Senate, and paved the road to war. More or less, these were the terms: the Cuban people would be independent, Spain would get out of Cuba, and the president would use military force to ensure compliance. A fourth resolution was added: "The United States does not have any wish to intervene in the Government of Cuba." Nevertheless, after a century, the United States still keeps the base at Guantánamo.

THE ROLE OF THE PRESS

As long as things were in the hands of the military after *Maine*'s explosion, everybody, including the American consul and the captain of the ship, agreed to talk only about the "accident." Two days after the accident things changed. On February 17, the *New York Journal* reported: "Destruction of the *Maine* was due to the enemy. It is believed the Spaniards got the *Maine* moored over one of the mines in the harbor. The brutal nature of the Spaniards. . . ." And a second edition of the newspaper said: "*Maine* broke in two by an infernal secret weapon of the enemy." There were two main newspapers that could claim the dubious merit of shaping the opinion of the enormous American middle class: the *New York Journal,* owned by the tycoon William Randolph Hearst, who inspired the famous Orson Wells movie *Citizen Kane,* and Joseph Pulitzer's *New York World.*

It was indeed Hearst who in 1898 characterized the leading role of the press in a modern state: "Newspapers shape and express public opinion. They suggest and control the laws. They declare wars." Hearst superbly sold the idea that imperialist aggression was philanthropic defense of a country subdued by colonial tyranny. The report to Hearst from war correspondent and famous artist Frederick Remington, is well known: "All quiet here. No disturbances. Like to come back because won't be any war." And Hearst's answer: "Stay there. You furnish the pictures and I'll furnish the war." The press distorted the truth and invented news with faked photographs. With headlines like "More than four hundred thousand Cubans dead in concentration camps," it was clear that respect for truth was subordinate to the need for sensationalist news to sell more newspapers than rival publishers could sell.

But what about the press in Spain? It is also true that certain newspapers were at the service of the oligarchy that ran big business in the colonies. Spain's business community also played the dangerous role of inducing a war to defend its economic interests. It is also true that many other newspaper articles were written by very ignorant men who did poor service to the truth and to Spain. To make things even worse, these journalists were often misled by inflated and erroneous data given to them by government authorities themselves about the force balance between the two countries, always underrating the adversary. This irresponsible press was almost unanimously in favor of a war with the United States, and this view was inflamed by blustering politicians.

THE LACK OF A STRATEGIC PLAN

Cuba was indeed an old, very complex problem due to a myriad of political, economic, social, and international issues. All the Spanish governments after 1868 failed to make consistent the decision to keep Cuba under the Spanish flag at any cost with the logical undertaking of adequate political, diplomatic, and military actions.

It was very well known that the United States wanted the island of Cuba, as well as Puerto Rico, and the Philippines, so the defense of the Spanish colonies needed permanent attention and appropriate naval forces. A naval policy in a country with such distant and worldwide interests should have included not only a program of naval construction, but also the provision of advanced support bases to guarantee the operational effectiveness of the force, as well as necessary alliances with other nations. Unfortunately, Spain did not have enough military power to get the attention and collaboration of other European powers. If the government had decided to keep the colonies it should have provided an adequate fleet. But the Navy was disregarded, ignored, and almost forgotten in the budgets. Long-lasting peace leads, in military terms, to degradation of warriors, weapons, and readiness. The direction of naval operations in an announced war was a difficult task for a country without a clear picture of what was needed, without a naval war college to provide the necessary studies, and with three different and distant theaters of operation: the Pacific, including the Philippine, Mariana, and Palau islands; the Atlantic, the Caribbean, and Cuba; and mainland Spain. A key factor in the Spanish defeat was the division of the fleet for these three different scenes of action.

On the contrary, the United States had concrete plans for a possible war with Spain. In 1884, Admiral Stephen B. Luce founded the Naval War College in Rhode Island precisely to study how to deal with a future war at sea.

THE WARNINGS OF ADMIRAL CERVERA

Admiral Pascual Cervera was the Chief of the Operations Squadron in the Caribbean. Since his appointment to the job, correspondence with Minister of the Navy Sigismundo Bermejo was sharp, forceful, and copious. The many documents left by Admiral Cervera showed how clear the dangers of war were to him, although very sadly he could not help to avoid them. He was forced to accomplish an impossible mission with loyalty, a sense of duty, and discipline. Cervera expressed his conviction many times to Minister Bermejo about the lack of readiness of ships and guns and about a complete lack of direction, instructions, or a war campaign plan. He demanded information on the enemy's deployment, intentions, and objectives. He asked for maps. The answers he received were always vague, idealistic, and in no way adjusted to reality. Cervera knew his squadron would be defeated if ordered to go to the Caribbean. The government ignored his warnings.

The strategic mistakes in planning a naval war are costly. There was no real preparation for war and the lack of a strategic plan was obvious. The government of Spain did not know what to do with the squadron of

Cervera. The admiral, conscious of his naval inferiority, was always in favor of protection of the Spanish mainland. He thought sending the squadron to Puerto Rico would be nonsense because of the lack of logistic support on the island (no shipyard, spare parts, coal, or water). To put the squadron in Santiago would be to put it in a mousetrap.

Minister Bermejo finally ordered the immediate sailing of the squadron to Cabo Verde to protect a squadron of torpedo boats whose destination was Puerto Rico. These boats were intended to protect the island, even though it was not actually threatened. Regarding Cervera's fleet, Mahan said: "He and his four brave ships were sentenced inexcusably by madness or false national pride manifested in a political pressure deaf to all professional judgement and military experience, and were abandoned to their fate." Historian Fernandez Almagro observed that only a Shakespeare could think of a more dramatic situation than the one Admiral Cervera found himself in.

BALANCE OF NAVAL POWER

The U.S. Navy was then by all means superior to the Spanish Navy. The U.S. naval command organized two squadrons with enough combat power to face the squadron Spain might have sent to attack U.S. harbors on the East Coast. This was a remote possibility, but it frightened North American civilians. Official authorities and the press in Spain misled the public about the real combat power of the Spanish Navy. For instance, on March 11, after the accident of the battleship *Maine,* the press office of the Navy published an "official list" of Spanish ships that included 17 protected cruisers, 20 unprotected cruisers, and 80 gunboats. Nothing was further from reality. The U.S. Navy boasted 6 battleships, 2 armored cruisers, 10 protected (partly armored) cruisers, and a number of gunboats, against a Spanish fleet of 5 cruisers, a few destroyers, and some lesser craft. Readiness of ships and guns was very much in favor of the United States; the range of the gunnery and fire density capability was also a great advantage for the U.S. ships. We could say that the combat power of the Spanish Navy in 1898 was inappropriate to Spain's political-strategic reality. It was degraded in general terms, inefficient in units and weapons, and insufficient to show and defend the flag in those circumstances.

DEPLOYMENT AND WAR

The Philippines was always low in the attention and priorities of Minister Bermejo. Cuba was closer—only four thousand miles! (The U.S. Navy was only 95 miles from Cayo Hueso.) Without intermediate support bases and a proper supply of coal, it was impossible to send reinforcement to the

Philippines. So, the general situation was this: defense of the Caribbean islands by Cervera's squadron, the Philippines abandoned to its fate, and Spain's mainland left almost unprotected.

The period of time between the explosion of the *Maine* and the declaration of war was very well employed by the United States to prepare for war and to deploy the naval forces. The first moves were to establish a blockade off the northern coast of Cuba by the squadron of Admiral William T. Sampson, just one day after the declaration of war, and to carry out a bombardment of Matanzas on April 27. In the meantime, Commodore George Dewey, with a squadron of 4 protected cruisers, 1 smaller cruiser, and 1 gunboat, got underway from Hong Kong for the island of Luzon in the Philippines. On May 1, 1898, this squadron destroyed the Spanish force of 2 unprotected cruisers, 4 gunboats, and 1 sloop that Rear Admiral Montojo gathered in Cavite, close to Manila.

Broadly speaking, the U.S. squadron was superior, but it is true that the Spanish did not attempt to take advantage of the coastal guns of 200 millimeter, perhaps because they were not operational, like most of the material in the islands. It is also true that the U.S. squadron was operating 7,000 miles from its mainland, but very much supported by the "neutral" British in Hong Kong. The use of tactical delaying maneuvers, or even the use of mines (which never arrived), could have been considered.

In the middle of the battle, Dewey was concerned because no Spanish ship seemed to be completely knocked out. Dewey debated whether to continue the action at the risk of running out of ammunition (he had already fired 6,000 rounds, which registered 139 hits). Montojo, with a poor evaluation of the situation, assisted him by ordering the scuttling of the Spanish ships. Regarding Montojo's complaint about the readiness of his ships and guns, Madrid responded in a peculiar way: "As I can not send any reinforcement I do hope your zeal and activity will substitute for the deficiencies." To quote my friend and former boss as Supreme Allied Commander, Atlantic, General John J. Sheehan: "Hope is not a military question."

The naval battle of Cavite was somewhat of a gunnery exercise for the U.S. ships. Wisely, Dewey put his ships at such a distance that no ships or coastal batteries could answer his fire. He executed the operation almost in a businesslike manner. The Spanish side of the battle was a pathetic parade of Quixotic courage. Spain suffered 77 dead and 233 wounded; the United States suffered 7 wounded officers and men.

Annexation of the Philippines was not in the plans for the United States, but Great Britain suggested doing so to avoid Germany's establishment of bases in the area. After the battle of Cavite, Germany sent one squadron to protect "German interests." The annexation may have also resulted in part from the insistence of Methodist missionaries. McKinley confessed to them that he had reached his decision by God's inspiration during a prayer to protect and instruct the Filipinos. The President had tasted the forbidden fruit and had been seduced by the discreet charms of imperialism.

The Tagalogs did not appreciate the white man's good will. They took charge of their own government. Some Filipinos made a fatal assumption: they thought they were to be free. But when the United States failed to leave the islands, they rose up in an insurrection that ended only after three years, the death of 600,000 Filipinos in a severe repression, and the capture of their leader, Emilio Aguinaldo. The country was finally freed in 1948.

What about Cervera? Cervera came to a paradoxical point of no return when on May 12 Minister Bermejo sent a message to him in Martinique: "Circumstances have changed since your departure. In addition to your instructions you may consider to come back to the Mainland, if you think your Squadron can not operate successfully . . . etc." Cervera received the message only after his arrival in Santiago. Following a southern approach, Cervera entered Santiago on May 19, far from the eyes of Sampson's ships, which were patrolling the waters between Cuba and Haiti.

The situation in Santiago was far from appropriate for basing the squadron there: very feeble coastal defenses; army troops of the garrison exhausted after many years of war; lack of food and medicines. After much deliberation, Cervera decided to stay in Santiago and to reinforce the garrison. This decision was subject then and afterwards to much discussion. Maybe he could have chosen Havana instead of Santiago, or departed the bay by night and in rough seas. One thing was sure, even in the best case of avoiding the blockade of Admiral Winfield Scott Schley, they could not go much farther than Puerto Rico, where the squadron would be completely out of support and again blockaded. As Charlie Brown has said: "Today I have made 100 decisions—all of them wrong."

Many factors can help account for Spain's defeat, including strange government orders, lack of visible direction of the war, and jealousy between authorities. Finally, General Blanco, who was in charge of the naval forces in Cuba at the end of the war, ordered Cervera to embark marine riflemen and sailors and get underway. Blanco gave the order not knowing that American General William Shafter had sent a message to the secretary of war announcing that he would begin a retreat from Santiago because of casualties suffered at the battles of El Caney and San Juan. Blanco also ignored the fact that 3,700 Spanish troops had just entered Santiago to reinforce the garrison.

Forced to make a wrong exit, at the wrong moment, Cervera, nevertheless made a detailed plan of escape. He assigned his flagship, the *Maria Teresa,* a mission with the highest risk: to engage the American warship *Brooklyn* so the other ships of the squadron would have a chance to escape the blockade. On July 3, with the fatalism of a convicted man who takes the "lift to the scaffold," Cervera gave orders to get underway. I am not going to describe the battle, but suffice to say that Spanish casualties totaled 350 dead and 160 wounded. On the U.S. side there were 1 killed and 2 wounded.

Cervera's convictions came true in all respects. War against the United States could not have been won in any case. But if a coherent political plan had been developed when it was clear that the war was inevitable, it could have allowed the implementation of a prudent strategy. Operations could have been conducted that would have led, if not to victory, to making things more difficult for the United States and enabling Spain to speak louder at the negotiating table after the war.

On December 10, 1898, the Treaty of Paris was signed, marking the end of the Spanish empire and the birth of the American empire. The outcome was akin to a scene in a Woody Allen movie in which, after his divorce, a man observes to a friend: "I have come to an agreement with my wife: she gets everything." In the case of the Spanish-American War, the United States was the wife.

In sum, the war between the United States and Spain was inevitable and would have occurred even without the timely accident of the *Maine*. But the cause of the *Maine*'s sinking is now being put to rest. Many American naval scholars now conclude, as the Spanish Navy did a hundred years ago, that the ship was not destroyed and its sailors killed by Spanish action. That tragic event happened long ago.

Today we gather as fellow mariners and as members of the brotherhood of the sea to honor a great leader of the U.S. Navy. The renowned American bandleader Les Brown once said: "Shoot for the moon. Even if you miss it you will land among the stars." There was a man who aimed for the moon. And he not only hit the moon, but also the sun and the stars, and he is still there shining—Theodore Roosevelt. He served his country well and we honor him.

NOTES

1. H. G. Rickover, *How the Battleship* Maine *was Destroyed* (Washington: Naval History Division, 1976), 95.

REFERENCES

Addington, Larry H. *The Patterns of War since the Eighteenth Century* (Bloomington: University of Indiana Press, 1994).

Calhoun, Gordon. "Maine Remembered. The Day Book." Hampton Roads Naval Museum, Hampton, VA. Jan-Feb 1998.

Cerezo, Captain Richard (SN). *El Potencial Bélico de la Armada en 1898.*

Cervera Pery, Brigadiere General Juan. Director of the Revista de Historia Naval. *De la Conducta y Trayectoria del Almirante Cervera en la Guerra Naval del 98.* 1995.

Cohen, Stan. *Images of the Spanish American War: Apr-Aug 1898* (Missoula, MT: Library of Congress Pictorial Histories Publishing Co. Inc., 1997).

"Cuba Libre" by the Museum Sage. Hampton Roads Naval Museum, Hampton, VA. 1998.

Galan, J. Eslava, and D. Rojana Oretega. *La España del 98. El Fin de una Era* (Madrid: Editorial EDAF, 1997).

Gonzalez-Aller, Rear Admiral Jose I. (Spanish Navy). *La Crisis de España (1868–1874). La Marina de la Restauración (1874–1902).* Conference. 1978.

Mahan, Alfred T. *The Interest of America in Sea Power: Present and Future* (London: Sampson, Low Co., 1897).

Monteavaro, Miguel Angel Serrano. *La Libertad de Expresión durante la Guerra Hispano-Cubana-Norteamericana.*

De Ojeda, Jaime. Ambassador of Spain. *La Guerra del 98: Una Visión Americana. Claves de Razón Práctica.* 1998.

———. *Unwanted War: Dilemmas of Foreign Policy.* Presentation to the 1898 Georgetown University Seminar. Apr 2, 1998.

Rickover, Hyman G. *How the Battleship* Maine *was Destroyed* (Annapolis, MD: Naval Institute Press, 1976).

Seco Serrano, Carlos. *Hoy hace un siglo.* ABC, Feb 15, 1998.

Valcarcel, Dario. *España Europea. ¿Recuerdan al Maine?* ABC, April 21, 1998.

Vila Miranda, Admiral Carlos. *España y la Armada en las Guerras de Cuba* (Gijon, Spain: Fundación Alvargonzález, 1998).

Army-Navy Joint Operations in the Spanish-American War

Graham A. Cosmas

ARMY-NAVY JOINT OPERATIONS IN THE SPANISH-AMERICAN WAR are usually recalled in terms of conflict and confusion. The strident arguments between Major General William R. Shafter and Rear Admiral William T. Sampson at Santiago dominate the picture. Generations of undergraduates have been amused or appalled by the spectacle of the Army swimming its horses and mules ashore at Daiquiri and Siboney for lack of landing craft. In fact, the story is more complex. While interservice disputes occurred, as they have in every American war, in the field cooperation predominated over conflict. In spite of prewar unpreparedness and doctrinal and technological limitations, the U.S. Army and U.S. Navy, in the main, worked together effectively to project American power and achieve the nation's military and political objectives.[1]

The services entered the Spanish-American War with considerable prior experience in joint operations, typified by General Winfield Scott's landing at Vera Cruz in 1847. The extensive coastal and riverine operations of the Civil War had left a rich foundation of institutional memory, if little in the way of formal written doctrine, for the senior commanders of 1898, who almost to a man were veterans of the earlier conflict. During the decades after Appomattox, the Navy kept its hand in amphibious operations, with major landings of marines and sailors in Korea (1871); Alexandria, Egypt

(1882); and Panama (1885). In 1891, the Navy Department codified its doctrine for these operations in a set of formal instructions for its landing brigades. The instructions, drafted by a board that included an Army officer to advise on infantry tactics, covered such fundamentals as loading boats, formation and control of assault waves, command and control, fire support, and organization of the beach. The Navy thus entered the Spanish-American War with a rudimentary doctrine for ship-to-shore operations, although it had not conducted any joint landing exercises with the Army since 1865.[2]

The creative cadre of post–Civil War Army and Navy officers who were trying to prepare their services for the twentieth century shared many common assumptions and values and exchanged ideas. General William T. Sherman, founder of the Army's officer school system, was a close personal and professional friend of Rear Admiral Stephen B. Luce, who established the Naval War College. One of the first regular faculty members of Luce's college was Army Lieutenant Tasker H. Bliss. According to Ronald Spector, Bliss, in his lectures on military strategy and tactics, provided the fledgling naval school with "the link between the new military science as developed in the European staff schools and the naval officers who were to apply it to sea warfare." After the Spanish war, Bliss played an important role in establishing the Army War College.[3]

Army and Navy leaders of the period shared common assumptions about the shape and conduct of the nation's future wars. Given the absence of major rival land powers in North America, they envisioned maritime and colonial conflicts with European or Latin American nations. In such wars, the Navy's new steel battle fleet would carry the burden of offensive operations while the Army's coastal fortifications protected the fleet's bases and the principal seaports and Army expeditions followed up naval successes by capturing strategic pieces of enemy territory. Army and Navy thinking about a conflict with Spain over Cuba and, in the Navy's case, contingency planning, were based on these assumptions. Leaders of both services expected that if it came to war, the Navy would blockade Cuba, make a descent upon Manila, and seek to engage and destroy the Spanish fleet. The Army would make ready the coast defenses and organize an expeditionary force for whatever missions emerged from the course of events, most likely an attack on Havana.[4]

The Army and Navy entered the war with Spain with a well-established, if informal, doctrine for command and control of joint operations. Army and Navy commanders, once assigned their forces and objectives, customarily enjoyed wide latitude in their conduct of campaigns and cooperated as independent equals. If disagreements arose, they resolved them by negotiation, or failing that, referred them back up their respective chains of command for decision ultimately at presidential and cabinet levels. This method was typical of late-nineteenth-century America, a society still governed more by personal relationships and informal consensus than by bureaucratic hierarchy. At that time, Great Britain, the world's premier naval power, employed much the same approach, with the major difference that the Royal Navy provided and controlled all transport shipping, whereas in the United States the Army mostly procured its own troopships, landing boats, and other water craft.[5]

Army-Navy cooperation during the war with Spain must be viewed from three levels: strategic, operational, and tactical. At the strategic level, President William McKinley improvised an informal but workable national command system. From his White House "war room," he kept in touch with the War and Navy Departments and (via telegraph) with commanders in Cuba, Puerto Rico, and the Philippines. At periodic meetings with Secretary of the Navy John D. Long, Secretary of War Russell A. Alger, their senior uniformed advisers, and often representatives of other executive departments, McKinley set overall policy and coordinated service planning and conduct of campaigns.[6]

As the services had expected, war strategy was truly joint, with Army operations largely developing out of the course of naval events. The principal source of friction at the strategic level was the different rate of mobilization of the two services. The Navy was ready first, and the rapid progress of its operations kept the Army scrambling to keep up. For example, to ensure the destruction of Cervera's squadron at Santiago, the Army had to improvise a major expedition early in its mobilization, using the inadequate resources of its peacetime establishment. This fact accounts for most of the confusion and supply shortages that plagued Army forces in the Santiago campaign.[7]

At the level of the conduct of campaigns, the picture was mixed. At Santiago de Cuba, Admiral Sampson and General Shafter disagreed on the priority of objectives (the city and garrison versus Cervera's squadron) and the concept of operations (an advance along the shore to seize the harbor forts versus a drive inland to encircle Santiago). Once his troops were on shore, Shafter conducted operations without regard to the fleet until the battles of San Juan Hill and El Caney left him facing a Spanish inner line he considered too formidable to attack. Shafter then tried to persuade Sampson to risk his battleships in an assault on the harbor entrance, which the admiral refused to do. The resulting deadlock embittered interservice relations, both at the front and in Washington. However, the ultimate outcome could not have been more favorable if the Army and Navy had made concerted plans from the beginning. Shafter's seizure of the high ground overlooking the city forced Cervera out of the harbor to destruction in the naval battle of July 3. Two weeks later, the garrison, beleaguered by land and sea and faced with the prospect of a renewed assault, surrendered along with its satellite forces elsewhere in eastern Cuba.[8]

In Puerto Rico and the Philippines, the services worked together more smoothly. During the Puerto Rico campaign, the fleet adjusted readily to Major General Nelson A. Miles's last-minute change of landing place, helped Army forces secure their lodgment at Ponce, and provided gunfire support when requested. At Manila, Rear Admiral George Dewey and Major General Wesley Merritt conducted the most truly joint campaign of the war. Their final assault on Manila on August 13, although something of a sham battle designed to give the Spanish commander an excuse to surrender, involved close cooperation by the land and naval forces at every point.[9]

At the tactical level, interservice cooperation largely consisted of landing operations and naval gunfire support of Army troops in combat. In all these areas, the services labored under doctrinal and technological deficiencies. Ship-to-shore communication in these pre-radio days depended on signal flags and dispatch boats. Even though the troops on shore could make use of relatively sophisticated field telegraph and telephone systems, those systems stopped at the water's edge. If Army forces moved any distance inland, rapid communication with the fleet became out of the question. Even more crippling than primitive communications was the lack in both services of specialized craft for across-the-beach landings. To place men and materiel on shore, they relied on ships' boats, usually towed by Navy steam launches, plus assortments of lighters, small steamers, tugs, and whatever other water craft could be procured on the scene.

Naval gunfire support was limited by the absence in both services of doctrine, equipment, and training for indirect artillery fire controlled by forward observers. This meant that the fleet could provide support only when operations took place close to shore and within sight of the ships' gunners. Hence, naval gunfire could not be used in Shafter's attacks on San Juan Hill and El Caney, which were inland and out of observation of the fleet.[10]

Within these limitations, the services performed creditably. Convoy operations were straightforward. Army transports steaming under Navy escort were under the orders of the senior naval officer and customarily embarked Navy signal parties to maintain communications. These simple arrangements generally sufficed to keep flotillas together and in order.[11]

At Santiago de Cuba, with no prior rehearsals, Admiral Sampson's squadron and General Shafter's V Corps put together the largest landing operation of the war. They mounted diversions at various points to confuse the Spaniards and supported the actual disembarkation at Daiquirí and Siboney with ships' gunfire heavy enough, according to one participant, "to drive out the whole Spanish army in Cuba had it been there," which it was not. Over open beaches, using the squadron's boats and steam launches, the Army transports' lifeboats, and a few small Army steamers and lighters, the Army and Navy over about five days put ashore more than 17,000 troops with their artillery, supplies, wagons, and draft animals. Total losses in the operation were 2 soldiers drowned on the first day, about 30 horses and mules lost in swimming them ashore, a Navy cutter wrecked, and a number of other boats damaged by surf or collisions. It is worth noting that the naval officer in charge of the ship-to-shore movement, Captain Caspar Goodrich of the scout cruiser USS *St. Louis,* had observed the British amphibious assault at Alexandria, Egypt, in 1882 and helped develop the U.S. Navy's landing doctrine during the 1880s and early 1890s.[12]

The landings of troops in Puerto Rico and at Manila, which took place inside commodious harbors and employed large numbers of locally captured lighters and small craft, posed fewer challenges than that at Santiago and were carried out without major incidents. Conducted in all cases against lightly defended or undefended shorelines, the Spanish-American War landings were not true amphibious assaults, which Army and Navy authorities at the time considered infeasible against repeating rifles and breech-loading artillery. American commanders went to great lengths to avoid enemy defenses. General Miles changed his landing place in Puerto Rico when intelligence reports indicated that the Spaniards had concentrated troops at the original site.[13]

Whenever possible during operations in Cuba, Puerto Rico, and the Philippines, the Army requested, and the Navy provided, gunfire support for engaged troops. The integration of gunfire support with land maneuvers reached its highest point in the attack on Manila. In that engagement, General Merritt, under a plan worked out with Admiral Dewey, relied on the fire of warships, which steamed along the shore on the army's flank, to break up the Spanish defense in front of his troops. Merritt instructed his brigade commanders to advance only after the Navy shelling had driven the Spaniards from their entrenchments. Such coordination was possible because Dewey's vessels could maneuver close to shore and bring direct fire to bear on the Spanish works.[14]

During the siege of Santiago de Cuba, the Army and Navy attempted to bombard the city with indirect fire. Battleships anchored offshore lobbed shells over the hills into the city guided by Army observers in the trenches on San Juan Hill. These men reported the fall of the shots by telephone to the beach, from which flag signalers relayed the reports to the ships. During the main bombardment, on July 10, the ships fired 46 shells in two hours. For fear of hitting American troops, none of the shots was fired at the Spanish trenches encircling Santiago. The Army observers failed to see or hear the impact of 24 rounds. Others caused visible explosions and a few small fires. A survey after the city's surrender determined that the shelling had cratered several streets and destroyed or damaged over 50 buildings. Its effect, if any, in bringing about the Spanish surrender is unknown. The exercise served mainly to demonstrate the limitations of indirect fire under the conditions of 1898.[15]

Overall, the story of Army-Navy cooperation in the war with Spain was one of success. In spite of limited resources, insufficiencies in technology, weaknesses in doctrine, and personal and professional disagreements among commanders, the services together brought adequate force to bear to defeat Spain. The established nineteenth-century system of coordination and cooperation proved sufficient for the demands of a limited colonial war against a weak European power, and it met as well the requirements of the subsequent struggle against Aguinaldo's insurgents in the Philippines.

Because the system did not appear to be broken, no one really tried to fix it. Even though major command and staff reforms occurred in each service after the Spanish war, notably the creation of the Army general staff and the Chief of Naval Operations, no major changes took place in the joint system. The Army retained its sea transport service, and the Navy created its own amphibious infantry in the form of the Marine Corps advanced base force. In 1903, largely at the instigation of Secretary of War Elihu Root, the Army and Navy Departments did establish a joint board to work out war plans and deal with interservice issues. However, this body simply institutionalized the existing consultative approach. In the field, the principal of command by cooperation remained in effect and was codified in regulations issued by the joint board. Not until World War II would the United States, confronted with the need to conduct integrated land, sea, and air campaigns, finally create truly joint institutions for planning and command.[16]

Yet even in an era of highly institutionalized "jointness," remnants of the earlier system occasionally emerged. In Vietnam during the 1960s, the theater headquarters, Military Assistance Command, Vietnam, established a joint riverine force of Navy river transports and gunboats and an Army brigade to operate in the Mekong Delta. Unable to agree on a single commander for the force, the services settled for separate Army and Navy commanders working in cooperation, an arrangement that would have looked very familiar to the soldiers and sailors of 1898.[17]

NOTES

1. Unless otherwise noted, this paper is based on the author's more extended essay, "Joint Operations in the Spanish-American War," in James C. Bradford, ed., *Crucible of Empire: The Spanish-American War and Its Aftermath* (Annapolis, MD: Naval Institute Press, 1993), 102–26.

2. "Instructions for Infantry and Artillery, United States Navy," *U.S. Naval Institute Proceedings* 17 (1891): 569–744.

3. Ronald Spector, *Professors of War: The Naval War College and the Development of the Naval Profession* (Newport, RI: Naval War College Press, 1977), 28–29; see 14–17 for examples of Luce's interaction with Army reformers, notably Sherman and Lieutenant Colonel Emory Upton.

4. A typical Army view of service roles and missions in future war is in Lieutenant General John M. Schofield, *Forty-Six Years in the Army* (New York: The Century Company, 1897), 527–28. Planning for the war with Spain is covered in David F. Trask, *The War with Spain in 1898* (New York: Macmillan, 1981), 72–78, 88–91; and Graham A. Cosmas, *An Army for Empire: The United States Army in the Spanish-American War* (2nd ed.) (Shippensburg, PA: White Mane Publishing Co., Inc., 1994), 68–76.

5. The American command tradition is summarized in Rowena Reed, *Combined Operations in the Civil War* (Annapolis, MD: Naval Institute Press, 1978), xiv–xv. The British system is discussed in Brigadier General G. G. Aston, CB, *Letters on Amphibious Wars* (London: John Murray, 1911), 143–45; and Ensign Charles G. Rogers, USN, et al., "Operations in the British Navy and Transport Service during the Egyptian Campaign of 1882," *U.S. Naval Institute Proceedings* 8 (Jan 1883): 523–635.

6. McKinley's command system is described in Trask, *War with Spain*, 88–89.

7. The Army's mobilization difficulties and their relationship to strategy can be followed in Cosmas, *Army for Empire*, chaps. 3 and 4.

8. Cosmas, "Joint Operations," 109–10.

9. Ibid., 110–11. A detailed contemporary account of Army-Navy cooperation at Manila can be found in Lieutenant Carlos G. Calkins, USN, "Historical and Professional Notes on the Naval Campaign of Manila Bay in 1898," *U.S. Naval Institute Proceedings* 25, no. 2 (Jun 1899): 267–321; see especially 299–300, 304–6.

10. The lack of indirect fire doctrine in the Army is recounted in Boyd L. Dastrup, *King of Battle: A Branch History of the U.S. Army's Field Artillery* (Washington: U.S. Army Center of Military History, 1993), 140–41. A contemporary Army officer's view of the inability of naval gunfire to support maneuvering land forces can be found in Ltr., Matthew F. Steele to Mrs. Steel, Jun 28, 1898, Matthew F. Steele Papers, U.S. Army Military History Institute, Carlisle Barracks, Pennsylvania.

11. Cosmas, "Joint Operations," 112.

12. The basic orders for the landing can be found in U.S. War Department, *Annual Report of the Major General Commanding the Army to the Secretary of War, 1898* (Washington: 1898), 150; and U.S. Navy Department, *Annual Report of the Secretary of the Navy, 1898*, vol. 2, *Appendix to the Report of the Chief of the Bureau of Navigation* (Washington: 1898), 497–98; see also 683–88, 693; hereafter cited as *Bureau of Navigation Report*. Goodrich's background is discussed in Cosmas, "Joint Operations," 113.

13. Cosmas, "Joint Operations," 117.

14. A convenient summary of this operation is in Cosmas, *Army for Empire*, 241–43.

15. Navy reports on this operation are in *Bureau of Navigation Report*, 611–12, 621–23, and 629–30. For Army views, see Alger, *Spanish-American War*, 235. A British analysis of the limitations on naval indirect fire, based on the American experience at Santiago and that of the Japanese at Port Arthur, can be found in Aston, *Letters on Amphibious Wars*, 131–33.

16. Elihu Root, *Five Years of the War Department* (Washington: 1904), 334–35, describes creation of the Army-Navy Board. Early-twentieth-century command doctrine is discussed in Captain Wyatt I. Selkirk, "The Cooperation of Land and Sea Forces," *Journal of the Military Service Institution of the United States* 46 (Mar-Apr 1910): 317–19.

17. General George S. Eckhardt, *Command and Control, 1950–1969. Vietnam Studies* (Washington: Department of the Army, 1974), 78–80.

FIVE

THEODORE ROOSEVELT AND THE HERITAGE OF THE U.S. NAVY

JOHN A. GABLE

IN THE 1970S HISTORIAN DAVID MCCULLOUGH ASKED P. James Roosevelt, who is regarded as the head of the Oyster Bay branch of the Roosevelt family, if he thought there was any important facet of Theodore Roosevelt that had been neglected by TR's biographers. "Yes," P. James Roosevelt said. "No writer seems to have understood the degree to which he was part of a clan."[1]

Since then the study of the Roosevelts as a clan or tribe has become, and remains, an important field of work for historians. McCullough's *Mornings on Horseback,* published in 1981, winner of the National Book Award, was followed by Geoffrey Ward's detailed and brilliant two volumes on Franklin Delano Roosevelt, *Before the Trumpet* (1985) and *A First Class Temperament* (1989), which emphasize the family context of FDR's life. Studies of the family include Sylvia Morris's perceptive biography of Edith Kermit Roosevelt (1980), Peter Collier's controversial book on the Roosevelts (1994), Betty Boyd Caroli's *The Roosevelt Women* (1998), and Edward J. Renehan Jr.'s *The Lion's Pride* (1998), a book about the Sagamore Hill Roosevelts in World War I. Finally, the genealogy of the Roosevelt family, an indispensable research tool, was published by the Theodore Roosevelt Association in 1990.[2]

The Roosevelts have continued to promote their history through family reunions held every three years. The first reunion was held at Hyde Park in

1989. Among the current interests of the family is the Roosevelt Study Center in Middelburg, Zeeland, in the Netherlands, an institution for the study of U.S. history, opened in 1986 and dedicated to Theodore, Franklin, and Eleanor Roosevelt.[3]

It is now quite clear that the descendants of the Dutch immigrants Claes and Jannetje van Rosenvelt, who arrived in New Amsterdam in the 1640s, form a discernible and coherent whole. The Roosevelts in general display many common traits and there are constant themes throughout much of the family history. Whether this is the result of heredity or environment, nature or nurture, or more likely a combination of both, the Roosevelts are a group almost as distinct as any Native American tribe. This truth was obscured for many years by the bitter partisan feud between the Oyster Bay and Hyde Park branches of the Roosevelt family. Now that the feud has faded away, we can see that at all times, even during this civil war, the Roosevelts held to a common heritage.

The principal themes in this history of the Roosevelts may be briefly listed. First, since the eighteenth century, many Roosevelts have been involved in politics and public life. Second, many Roosevelts have been attracted to outdoor life on land, and have been hunters, explorers, naturalists, and conservationists. Third, Roosevelts have also been drawn to the sea. They have made a name in yachting circles, and they have been strongly linked to the Navy and naval affairs. Fourth, in both the Army and Navy the Roosevelts have made their mark, winning scores of combat medals; and during the Cold War, they turned to the intelligence community for avenues of service. Pacifists and vegetarians are not numerous in this tribe. Fifth, while Roosevelts have frequently been cursed on Wall Street, many in the family have been drawn to business, almost exclusively in investment rather than management. Sixth, as busy as Roosevelts have been running for public office, hunting on five continents, racing sailboats, and exploring the remote wilds, they have always found time to write books on subjects ranging from history to cooking. The Roosevelts have produced more books than any other family in American history. Finally, we find that the family has been drawn to what might be called innovation. Several Roosevelts were inventors, and many have been active in political, social, and economic reform.[4]

It is easy to see why historians and writers are drawn to the subject of the Roosevelt family: they are colorful and dramatic, as well as prodigious achievers, and their activities are linked to some of the most important topics in American and, indeed, world history. On *Time* magazine's recent list of the most important people of the twentieth century, the Roosevelts are the only family with more than one name. The list contained three Roosevelts: TR, FDR, and TR's niece and FDR's wife, Eleanor Roosevelt, who arguably was one of the most famous women of the twentieth century.[5]

Turning to one of the family interests, the Roosevelt naval heritage, we find that Theodore Roosevelt was the crucial and major formulator of the family tradition. Indeed, this is true of all of the family's thematic traditions with the very definite exception of investment. With each of the Roosevelt traditions or themes, TR is not the first in the field; he was influenced by and found direction from his family and he in turn inspired younger generations of the clan. But without question it was Theodore Roosevelt who was the most important Roosevelt in defining the family's interests in politics, nature, the sea, military service, writing, and innovative reform.

What were the family influences on Theodore Roosevelt's interest in ships, the sea, and the Navy? Nicholas Roosevelt (1767–1854), for example, is the true inventor of the steamboat, in the eyes of the Roosevelt clan. Be that as it may, or may not be, in 1812 he was certainly the first to take a steamboat down the Mississippi River.[6]

More important by far were Theodore Roosevelt's two uncles from Georgia, James Dunwody Bulloch (1823–1901) and Irvine Stephens Bulloch (1842–1898). "Uncle Jimmy" Bulloch was an admiral of the Confederate Navy, serving in Europe. He was the builder of the *Alabama,* and his much younger half brother, Irvine Bulloch, was a midshipman on the *Alabama,* who, TR relates, "fired the last gun discharged from her batteries in the fight with the *Kearsage.*" After the war, the uncles lived in exile in England; but they retained close links to TR and his family. With TR's encouragement, James Bulloch wrote his memoirs, *The Secret Service of the Confederate States in Europe,* 2 volumes published in London, 1883.[7]

Theodore Roosevelt's mother was Martha Bulloch from Roswell, Georgia. According to David McCullough, it is Martha Bulloch who changed the Roosevelts forever. With her colorful tales of a dashing, daring South, her romantic heritage, and her heroic brothers, who fought on the high seas while the Roosevelts sat in the offices of Roosevelt & Son counting their money and avoiding the Civil War, Martha Bulloch represented a lively infusion into the Roosevelt environment. When Ethel Roosevelt Derby, TR's daughter, met President Jimmy Carter in 1977, she said, "My father's mother came from Georgia, and we always said his Southern blood made all the difference."[8]

Another nautical influence operative in the Roosevelt family environment was sailing and yachting. Theodore Roosevelt's cousins and their descendents have played an important part in the history of American sailing. Oyster Bay, Long Island, is one of the most famous ports in the yachting world, and the Seawanhaka Corinthian Yacht Club on Centre Island, founded in 1871, is the oldest amateur yacht club in the United States. A long line of Roosevelts have been commodores, trustees, and racing champions at Seawanhaka. TR's cousin George E. Roosevelt (1887–1963) was commodore of both Seawanhaka and the New York Yacht Club. Franklin D. Roosevelt was a sailor all his life. He acquired his first boat, the *New Moon,* when he was 16. The Hyde Park Roosevelts did much sailing from their summer base on Campobello Island. In sum, sailing has been a major element in the Roosevelt environment for many generations.[9]

As is well known, the first of Theodore Roosevelt's many books was *The Naval War of 1812,* begun when he was a student at Harvard and published in 1882 when TR was 23. *The Naval War of 1812* is a classic still in print. The study became a textbook at the Naval War College, and in 1886 copies were placed on every ship in the U.S. Navy. Later Roosevelt was asked to write the section on the War of 1812 in the official history of the British Navy, edited by Sir William Laird Clowes, a high tribute to TR's status as a naval historian.[10]

Franklin D. Roosevelt's interest in the Navy also had a scholarly dimension. FDR collected naval prints, books, ship models, and other nautical items. Eventually his collection consisted of over 1,000 prints and paintings, 2,500 books (900 with catalog cards in FDR's longhand), and hundreds of manuscripts, pamphlets, letters, log books, and other items. Today a gallery in the Franklin D. Roosevelt Library at Hyde Park is dedicated to the display of materials from this collection.[11]

Theodore Roosevelt's relationship with Alfred Thayer Mahan has received much attention from historians. Roosevelt helped Mahan's career, but the influence of each man upon the other and the differences in their views remain the subject of some debate. Yet, it seems accurate to speak of them as part of the same naval tradition, and to say that together they gave the U.S. Navy an intellectual dimension that has been crucial in shaping the character of successive generations of naval officers. Admiral Mahan was a hero to Franklin D. Roosevelt. When the old man was muzzled by the Wilson administration in 1914, FDR sympathized, though to no avail. In 1940, President Franklin D. Roosevelt saw to it that the Navy appropriately honored the centennial of Mahan's birth.[12]

In 1897, Theodore Roosevelt became the first of five members of his family to hold the position of Assistant Secretary of the Navy. Although he served in that post for only a year (April 19, 1897 to May 6,1898), Theodore Roosevelt is probably the most famous Assistant Secretary of the Navy in history.

Geoffrey Ward has given us the most detailed account of Franklin D. Roosevelt's attempts to follow in TR's footsteps. Like TR, FDR served in the New York legislature, and when FDR was offered the post of Assistant Secretary of the Navy in Woodrow Wilson's administration, Franklin said, "I'd like it bully well!" TR wrote to FDR on March 18, 1913: "Dear Franklin: I was very much pleased that you were appointed as Assistant Secretary of the

Navy. It is interesting to see that you are in another place which I myself once held." A few weeks later TR sent FDR a warning: "I do not anticipate trouble with Japan, but it may come, and if it does it will come suddenly."[13]

Historians have not been particularly laudatory in their treatment of Franklin Roosevelt's years in the Navy Department, but one can hardly call the Wilson administration a friendly environment for Rooseveltian naval policy. FDR resigned from the Navy Department in 1920 to run for vice president, another post TR had held. But of course FDR went down to defeat in 1920.

In 1921 Theodore Roosevelt Jr. was appointed Assistant Secretary of the Navy. His tenure was distinguished by his able work on naval arms limitations, and his role in exposing the Teapot Dome mess. Theodore Roosevelt Jr. resigned from the Navy Department in 1924 to run for governor of New York. Al Smith defeated him.[14]

It is in 1920 and then 1924 that we see the bitter breach between the Hyde Park and Oyster Bay branches of the Roosevelt family. Here were two Roosevelts fighting over TR's mantle, his nephew by marriage and his son. In 1920, Theodore Jr. campaigned against FDR, and in 1924, Eleanor Roosevelt campaigned against TR Jr. This is long before the New Deal, and the split was not over issues but simply about two ambitious men who got in each other's way.

Theodore Jr. was replaced in the Navy Department by Theodore Douglas Robinson, "Teddy Douglas," the son of President Theodore Roosevelt's sister, Corinne Roosevelt Robinson. Theodore Douglas Robinson (1883–1934) served in the Navy Department from 1924 to 1929. When FDR became President, he appointed his distant cousin Henry Latrobe Roosevelt (1879–1936) as Assistant Secretary of the Navy. Henry Latrobe Roosevelt was descended from "Steamboat" Nicholas Roosevelt. Henry Latrobe Roosevelt served from 1933 until his death in 1936. Both Teddy Douglas Robinson and Henry Latrobe Roosevelt were well qualified for the appointments they held. Robinson had been Progressive Party chairman of New York, and had served in both houses of the New York legislature. Henry Latrobe Roosevelt was a graduate of Annapolis, and had been a lieutenant colonel in the Marine Corps.

Since the 1930s the Roosevelt tradition in the Navy has continued. Franklin and Eleanor's sons Franklin D. Roosevelt Jr. and John A. Roosevelt served in the Navy in World War II while their son James was in the Marine Corps. President Theodore Roosevelt's grandsons Theodore Roosevelt III and Cornelius Roosevelt were in the Navy in World War II, and Theodore Roosevelt IV was a frogman in Vietnam.

There has been a definite aviation component to the Roosevelt naval tradition. In 1898, Assistant Secretary of the Navy Theodore Roosevelt wrote a memo to Secretary John D. Long reporting on the "flying machine" developed by his friend, Professor S. P. Langley. "The machine has worked," TR wrote. "It seems worth while for this Government to try whether it will not work on a large enough scale to be of use in the event of war."[15] As President, TR purchased planes from the Wright brothers for the Army. FDR and Theodore Roosevelt Jr. supported naval aviation. As President in 1933, FDR took $238 million from emergency relief Public Works Administration funds and constructed 2 aircraft carriers, 4 cruisers, 20 destroyers, 4 submarines, and 2 gunboats. The two aircraft carriers were the *Yorktown* and the *Enterprise.*[16]

Given TR's early vision of naval aviation, it is appropriate that today the Navy includes the carrier USS *Theodore Roosevelt* (CVN-71), commissioned in 1986. The Theodore Roosevelt Association has been the support organization for the carrier since pre-commissioning days.

TR also supported development of the submarine. Most naval historians know about the historic day in 1905 when the President went down in and piloted the submarine *Plunger*. It was TR who recognized that service on a submarine is something special that deserves special recognition in pay.[17]

Theodore Roosevelt was one of the founders of the Navy League of the United States, and FDR was also a great supporter of the Navy League, an organization that has stood by the Navy in good times and bad. It is therefore appropriate that the New York Council of the Navy League established the annual Theodore and Franklin D. Roosevelt Naval History Prize, awarded for what is judged to be the best book on American naval history published during the preceding year. The first recipient of the prize was Ronald H. Spector in 1986 for his book *Eagle Against the Sun*. The 1999 award was to Edward J. Marolda and Robert J. Schneller for their work, *Shield and Sword: The United States Navy and the Persian Gulf War*. Over the years the panel of judges has included such historians as Dr. Dean C. Allard, Professor K. Jack Bauer, Colonel Charles Brower, and Dr. John B. Hattendorf. The New York Council of the Navy League also awards a Roosevelt Gold Medal "for extraordinary contributions through science to the security of America." The medal honors TR and FDR, and was first awarded in 1986, the same year the book prize was established.[18]

One of the less well-known components of the Roosevelt naval tradition has been the subject of naval arms limitations. Theodore Roosevelt Jr., as Assistant Secretary of the Navy, working with Secretary of State Charles Evans Hughes, was much involved in the naval talks and negotiations of the early 1920s. In this work Ted was following, not departing from, his father's example. Theodore Roosevelt as President was the first world leader to call for convening what became the Second Hague Peace Conference. The egotism of Tsar Nicholas II made it necessary to give him the official and public credit for calling the conference, but the record is clear about TR's role. One of the main reasons TR wanted to hold the conference was to bring about naval arms limitations. TR had no success in this objective, as we know, but his strong desire to curtail the naval arms race shows that he had priorities in the direction of peace.[19]

Turning to the presidential administrations of Theodore Roosevelt and Franklin D. Roosevelt, we find much that is controversial. But in each case the proverbial bottom line is most impressive! Whereas once upon a time writers simply celebrated President Theodore Roosevelt's historic creation of the modern Navy, today historians are more likely to note the many problems that can be seen when we take a second look at the Navy under TR. There were problems in naval technology, and nobody lasted long enough as Secretary of the Navy to get a firm grip on policy.[20]

As for President Franklin Roosevelt's record, there are endless topics for debate, mostly in the area of strategy. The questions associated with the Pearl Harbor attack and Yalta remain unanswered for much of the general public, in spite of the books that have been written. Pearl Harbor sometimes seems like the Kennedy assassination, in that it won't go away, and Yalta remains an emotional issue for many people. FDR is the most popular president of this century. Yet some historians, such as Frederick W. Marks, attack virtually every aspect of FDR's foreign and military policy. Marks sees no continuity at all, and much contrast, between TR and FDR.[21]

Looking in the direction of TR, it is significant that certain images from his presidency do not fade with the passage of time. The scenes of the transit of the remains of John Paul Jones from France and the burial at Annapolis, and all those many pictures of the Great White Fleet leaving Virginia and returning after circling the globe, retain power for the beholder. They do not fade but remain part of the national consciousness. Moreover, the growth in size of the U.S. Navy under TR from sixth to second or third place set a standard of American greatness and power that has influenced world history almost beyond measure in this the "American Century." As for FDR, no matter what else may be said with accuracy or fairness in criticism of him, he was the Commander in Chief who won a two-ocean war, and that puts him in a class all by himself, above all other presidents.

There have always been books about Roosevelts in this century, but today there is an increasing emphasis on the family dynamics of this remarkable and lively group of people. What we are finding out is that there is coherence in this clan, a tribal tradition and environment that is a historical fact of considerable significance. The Roosevelt tribal tradition includes, as I have noted, involvement in politics and government, a wide-ranging engagement with wild places and nature, a continual connection with the sea, a mandate for military service, the habit of publishing books, and a tendency to be involved in reform and innovation.

The Roosevelt nautical tradition has not as yet been adequately considered or studied as such, and if it is ignored the history of both the Roosevelt family and the Navy will be incomplete. For many years Theodore Roosevelt's birthday, October 27, was celebrated as "Navy Day," and that fact and its implications should not be forgotten by those who go down to the sea in books.

I leave you with the image of two aging men wearing Navy surplus cloaks, as portrayed in Philip de Laszlo's famous painting of Theodore Roosevelt, and in countless photos and films of Franklin Roosevelt. These two presidents are often seen as icons of the "American Century," and a part of their iconography are those naval capes. Let this not be forgotten, and let the significance of this be noted by those who seek to understand TR, FDR, and the Roosevelt naval tradition, and the history of the American navy.

NOTES

1. David McCullough, *Mornings on Horseback* (New York: Simon and Schuster, 1981), 12.
2. McCullough, *Mornings on Horseback;* Geoffrey C. Ward, *A First-Class Temperament: The Emergence of Franklin Roosevelt* (New York: Harper & Row, 1989); Sylvia Jukes Morris, *Edith Kermit Roosevelt: Portrait of a First Lady* (New York: Coward, McCann & Geoghegan, 1980); Peter Collier with David Horowitz, *The Roosevelts: An American Saga* (New York: Simon and Schuster, 1994); Betty Boyd Caroli, *The Roosevelt Women* (New York: Basic Books, 1998); Edward J. Renehan Jr., *The Lion's Pride: Theodore Roosevelt and His Family in Peace and War* (New York: Oxford University Press, 1998); *The Roosevelt Family in America: A Genealogy,* published in the *Theodore Roosevelt Association Journal* XVI, nos. 1, 2, 3 (1990).
3. See "Roosevelt Family Reunion in North Dakota," *Theodore Roosevelt Association Journal* XXII, nos. 1 and 2 (Fall 1997): 28–29; Cornelius A. van Minnen, ed., *Ten More Years! A Celebration of the Roosevelt Study Center's Tenth Anniversary on 19 September 1996* (Middleburg, Netherlands: Roosevelt Study Center: 1997).
4. See Nathan Miller, *The Roosevelt Chronicles* (Garden City, NY: Doubleday & Co., 1979).
5. *Time,* Apr 13, 1998.
6. Miller, *Roosevelt Chronicles,* 92–105.
7. TR, quoted from Theodore Roosevelt, *Theodore Roosevelt: An Autobiography* (New York: Macmillan, 1913), 15–16; on the Bullochs, see Clarece Martin, "The Southern Heritage of Theodore Roosevelt," in Natalie A. Naylor, Douglas Brinkley, and John Allen Gable, eds., *Theodore Roosevelt: Many-Sided American* (Interlaken, NY: Heart of the Lakes Publishing, 1992), 35–44;

James D. Bulloch, *The Secret Service of the Confederate States in Europe* (London: Richard Bentley and Son, 1883), 2 vols.

8. McCullough, *Mornings on Horseback,* 40–48.

9. Otis L. Graham Jr. and Meghan R. Wander, eds., *Franklin D. Roosevelt: His Life and Times, An Encyclopedic View* (Boston: G. K. Hall, 1985), 382–83.

10. Edward K. Eckert, introduction to Theodore Roosevelt, *The Naval War of 1812* (Annapolis, MD: Naval Institute Press, 1987), xi–xxxii.

11. Graham and Wander, *Franklin D. Roosevelt: An Encyclopedic View,* 280–81.

12. Eckert, *The Naval War of 1812,* xxx–xxxi; on FDR and Mahan, see Renehan, *Lion's Pride,* 59–62.

13. "Bully well," Geoffrey Ward in Graham and Wander, *FDR: An Encyclopedic View,* 374–75; TR to FDR, Mar 18, 1913, *The Letters of Theodore Roosevelt,* ed. Elting E. Morison, et al. (Cambridge: Harvard University Press, 8 vols. 1951–1954), vol. 7, 714; TR to FDR, May 10, 1913, in Ibid., 729. Also see James L. Golden, "FDR's Use of the Symbol of TR in the Formation of his Political Persona and Philosophy" in Naylor, Brinkley, and Gable, *Theodore Roosevelt,* 577–94.

14. On Theodore Roosevelt Jr. as Assistant Secretary of the Navy, see Mrs. Theodore Roosevelt Jr., *Day Before Yesterday: The Reminiscences of Mrs. Theodore Roosevelt, Jr.* (Garden City, NY: Doubleday, 1959), chaps. 15, 16.

15. TR to John D. Long, Mar 25, 1898, *Letters of Theodore Roosevelt,* vol. 1, 799.

16. Kenneth J. Hagan, *This People's Navy: The Making of American Sea Power* (New York: The Free Press, 1991), 283.

17. TR to Charles Bonaparte, Aug 28, 1905, *Letters of Theodore Roosevelt,* vol. 4, 1323–25.

18. "Roosevelt Naval History Prize Goes to Co. Alexander," *Theodore Roosevelt Association Journal* XXI, no. 3 (Fall 1996): 24–25; "New York Navy League," *Theodore Roosevelt Association Journal* XIV, no. 1 (Winter 1998): 19.

19. Barbara W. Tuchman, *The Proud Tower: A Portrait of the World Before the War, 1890–1914* (New York: Macmillan, 1966), 274, 277–82.

20. See Robert William Love Jr., "TR's Big Stick: Roosevelt and the Navy, 1901–1909," in Naylor, Brinkley, and Gable, *Theodore Roosevelt,* 317–28.

21. Frederick W. Marks III, *Wind Over Sand: The Diplomacy of Franklin Roosevelt* (Athens: University of Georgia Press, 1988); Frederick W. Marks III, "Theodore Roosevelt, American Foreign Policy, and the Lessons of History," in Naylor, Brinkley, and Gable, *Theodore Roosevelt,* 391–410.

SIX

ROOSEVELT'S NAVAL THINKING BEFORE MAHAN

LIEUTENANT COMMANDER HENRY J. HENDRIX II, USN

As WE OBSERVE THE CENTENNIAL ANNIVERSARY of the Spanish-American War, we have the opportunity to reexamine history, that collective memory that defines us as a nation. With that opportunity comes a responsibility to challenge that memory, to sift fact from myth, to seek the truth. In a century that gave rise to "revisionist history," there is an imperative to separate fact from interpretative fiction. One memory, which merits review, surrounds the nature of the relationship between Theodore Roosevelt and the gifted naval strategist and historian, Captain Alfred Thayer Mahan.

Perhaps no other man can claim such influence upon the events of this century as Theodore Roosevelt. If, as the publisher Henry Luce said, the twentieth century is the "American Century," and we accept that this achievement stems from the nation's active leadership of the international order, then we must give credit to the man who almost single-handedly persuaded the American people to drop their inward focus of the nineteenth century and take up an international vision. While Theodore Roosevelt's position as the sponsor of the modern American fleet and as the prime advocate of the policy of international engagement is strong, there is a popular belief that these policies resulted from the influence of Mahan on Roosevelt. Some have reduced Roosevelt to a Mahanian sycophant, describing TR as a "disciple" to Mahan's "prophet."[1] It is the intent of this paper to demonstrate that nothing could be further from the truth. Primary sources amply illustrate that Roosevelt grasped the fundamentals of sea power well before Captain Mahan published *The Influence Sea Power Upon History, 1660–1783* in 1890.[2]

Mahan's classic work draws its distinction from the succinct manner in which the author distills the elements of sea power, and then demonstrates sea power's essential role in national greatness. Mahan's six elements of sea power are: 1) geographic position, 2) physical conformation, 3) extent of territory, 4) number of population, 5) character of the people, and 6) character of the government (including the national institutions).[3] While a nation need not be well endowed in all categories, it must be in most if it wishes to compete in the dynamic arena of power projection from the seas. These elements appeared in Mahan's lectures at the Naval War College, compiled in 1890. This date shall serve as the base by which Theodore Roosevelt's claim to uninfluenced mastery of the concepts of sea power shall be measured.

EARLY INFLUENCES

Childhood defines each individual, forming traits and attributes as unique as any fingerprint. Born just prior to the Civil War, Roosevelt developed in tumultuous times that defined him to the end of his days. TR descended on his father's side from a line of well-to-do Dutch merchants who "for . . . seven generations from father to son lived . . . on Manhattan Island."[4] These blue-blooded glassmakers, however, did not wholly define the character of the young boy. The salt in the blood of his mother's line also directed the destiny of young "Teedie."

Martha "Mittie" Bulloch Roosevelt epitomized the classic Southern belle. Married to Theodore Roosevelt Sr. in 1863, she left a plantation home in Roswell, Georgia, to reside with him in New York, but never left her culture or sympathies behind. Her children later remembered Mittie lying immobile during the Civil War, a physical symbol of the agony racking the nation. Theodore Sr., a "gentleman," perhaps out of sympathy to his wife (or perhaps because it was what rich businessmen of the day did), paid a substitute to take his place in the Union line. His sympathies, however, were never in question. He traveled between New York and Washington, D.C., raising funds for Union charities.

Mrs. Roosevelt's brothers, James Dunwody Bulloch and Irvine Bulloch, both served in the Confederate Navy with distinction. James, after early success as a blockade-runner, masterminded the construction and launching of the famed Southern commerce raider CSS *Alabama,* ultimately attaining the rank of rear admiral. His younger brother, Irvine, served on board *Alabama* as a midshipman, and gained distinction as the man who "fired the last gun discharged from her batteries in the fight with the *Kearsarge*."[5] In the days following Lee's surrender, both men visited the Roosevelt home incognito prior to taking up residence in England where, as un-reconstructed rebels, they exiled themselves for the rest of their lives.[6]

While young Theodore's loyalties during the Civil War mirrored his father's (he would often pray loudly for the ruination of the rebellious south)[7] he nevertheless held his maternal uncles in high esteem. While the war was never spoken about (mother and father, for the sake of the marriage, had agreed to disagree), the children often observed Mittie and her mother and sister preparing care packages bound for the South via blockade runners.[8] Mittie spoke glowingly to the sickly young boy of her brothers, recounting their adventures. His mother, he later recalled, told tales "about ships, ships, ships, and fighting of ships till they sank into the depths of my soul."[9]

Young Roosevelt visited the subjects of these tales twice during his adolescence. During his tenth year, and later at age 14, his father took the family on year-long tours of Europe and Africa. Each trip began and ended in England, allowing Mittie to see her brothers. On each visit, Teedie sat, awed, at the feet of the mythological heroes of his bedtime stories, absorbing firsthand the salt of their briny tales. Their stories ignited his imagination. Restricted as he often was by childhood asthma, TR used books as the sustaining fuel of this early fire.

A prominent example of this influence is the nineteenth-century book by Royal Navy Captain Frederick Marryatt, *Mr. Midshipman Easy*. Cited numerous times in Roosevelt's autobiography, it is a tale of a young officer torn between the excessive liberty of childhood and the discipline of the navy, maturing in the age of sail. The book details how the Nelsonian navy helped expand and maintain the British empire. Marryatt, drawing upon his personal experiences as a captain of a ship-of-the-line, describes a young man's efforts to become a good naval officer, worthy of service in the far-flung empire. Roosevelt later admitted "reveling in Marryatt's *Midshipmen Easy*."[10] This appreciation of the age of sail soon found expression in his adult intellectual pursuits.

THE NAVAL WAR OF 1812

Roosevelt's *The Naval War of 1812* remains a singular achievement in historical literature, more than a hundred years after its appearance. First it is well written. *The Naval War of 1812* stands with the works of Winston Churchill and Charles Dickens in its faultless sentence structure and precise grammar. Second, it is a classic of history, regarded still as a comprehensive narrative on the subject. Such an accomplishment is the aim of every serious historian, and is remarkable in one only 23 years old.

As a prerequisite to graduating with distinction, Roosevelt wrote an honor's thesis on a subject that had fascinated him since childhood: the sea and its impact upon national power. He drew heavily upon primary source materials supplied by the Library of Congress, the Navy Department, and the British government. At one point, Roosevelt found himself so overwhelmed with information that he doubted his ability to mold the work into presentable form. "I have plenty of information now," he wrote, "but I can't get it into words; I am afraid it is too big a task for me."[11] Visiting his uncle, Irvine Bulloch, in Liverpool, England, helped the young writer organize his materials and overcome his anxiety.[12]

The Naval War of 1812 is primarily an operational history of the naval aspects of the conflict between the United States and its former colonial master. Even the author found his first two chapters "so dry that they . . . made a dictionary light reading."[13] But the rest of the book presented a blow-by-blow recounting of great sea battles, with vivid descriptions of the personalities involved, and the preparations that either ensured victory or defeat. Tactical considerations surrounding fleet actions, one-on-one duels, and commerce raiding are related in great detail. How a civilian barely out of college could grasp the technicalities of these great clashes still serves to amaze. Friends later remembered arriving at the Roosevelt home for a night of socializing only to find TR standing before his mantle with deck logs, models of ships, and cannon strewn before him, lost in the visualization of bygone battles.[14]

TR's battle analysis was less important than his strategic insight. Not satisfied to simply recount the frigate and sloop conflicts of "Mr. Madison's War," Roosevelt extracted historical lessons and applied them to contemporary events. Roosevelt's narrative reflected his intuitive grasp of the elements of sea power years before Mahan reported as a new instructor to the Naval War College in Newport, Rhode Island.

Permeating TR's book is the proposition that a coastal state with a western and northern frontier exposed to enemy incursion is geographically vulnerable. English soldiers and their Native American allies conducted multiple campaigns along the Saint Lawrence River, throughout the Great Lakes, and into the Ohio Valley. Opposing these forces, early on, was a disorganized militia that ran as often as it stood. Only the Navy's control of the vital waterways protected the periphery of the United States. Chapters devoted to the campaigns on the Great Lakes state emphatically that the main mission of the American flotilla there was "to assist in repelling an invasion of the United States."[15]

Roosevelt highlights the importance of overseas bases for American ships by detailing the Odyssey-like voyage of USS *Essex*. "An American ship," he stated, "was at a serious disadvantage in having no harbor of refuge away from home"[16] when sailing far from U.S. waters in search of the enemy. While crediting American captains for their audacity in sailing "almost in sight of the British coast and right in the tract of the merchant fleets,"[17] he also understood that "the material results [of the cruises] were not very great."[18] He knew that the small U.S. Navy could have only limited impact on Great Britain's war effort.

Roosevelt also comprehended the effect that physical conformation and extent of territory (length of the coastline, the presence of good harbors and other safe havens for shipping, access to the interior, etc.) have on sea power. Roosevelt's grasp of these fundamentals stands out in his analysis of the tactical challenges facing the British in late 1813, when their fleet had effectively bottled up American warships in their homeports:

> As New England's loyalty to the Union was, not unreasonably, doubted abroad, her coasts were at first troubled but little. A British squadron was generally kept cruising off the end of Long Island Sound, and another off Sandy Hook. . . . Frigates and sloops kept skirting the coasts of New Jersey, the Carolinas, and Georgia. Delaware Bay no longer possessed the importance it had during the Revolutionary War, and as the only war vessels in it were miserable gun-boats, the British generally kept but a small force on that station. Chesapeake Bay became the principle scene of their operations; it was there that their main body collected, and their greatest efforts were made.[19]

This passage presented a succinct description of the extent of the American coastline, the strategic ports, and the nature of America's maritime defenses.

Roosevelt admired the British blockading ships, likening them to "hawks" hovering offshore day-in, day-out, even in the worst weather. In contrast, he deprecated the small gunboats provided by the U.S. government for the defense of America's vital harbors. Even though a landsman, Roosevelt appreciated the inadequacy of these "bad craft" for defending the Chesapeake. He placed blame for the enemy's dominance in the Chesapeake and burning of Washington, the nation's new capital, on the lack of proper naval resources.[20]

The Naval War of 1812 also reflects Roosevelt's clear understanding, as Mahan would later have, of the importance to sea power of a maritime-oriented populace.[21] His contention that the size of a population is not as important as the proportion involved in seafaring pursuits predates Mahan's similar conclusion. TR observed:

> The old Massachusetts town of Salem was then one of the main depots of the East India trade; the Baltimore clippers carried goods into the French and German ports with small regard to the [British] blockade; New Bedford and

Sag Harbor fitted out whalers for the Arctic seas as well as for the South Pacific; the rich merchants of Philadelphia and New York sent their ships to all parts of the world; and every small port had some craft in the coasting trade. On the New England seaboard but few of the boys would reach manhood without having made at least one voyage to the Newfoundland Banks after codfish; and in the whaling towns of Long Island it used to be a saying that no man could marry till he struck his whale. The wealthy merchants of the large cities would often send their sons on a voyage or two before letting them enter their counting-houses. Thus it came about that a large portion of our population was engaged in seafaring pursuits.[22]

Roosevelt believed that America at the dawn of the nineteenth century was a nation largely dependent upon maritime trade for subsistence, an appreciation he felt the administration of Thomas Jefferson did not have prior to the War of 1812—with dire results for war readiness.

A strong maritime sector did not necessarily produce great fighting sailors. Roosevelt, an adherent of racially based Social Darwinist thinking, observed that even though Portugal, Spain, and France possessed strong seagoing commercial sectors, these nations failed to produce great naval warriors on a par with Nelson or Farragut. In fact, TR found the American national character superior even to that of the British. America, in Roosevelt's mind, was the font of self-reliance and independent thought. He sang the praises of America's sailors:

> There was no better seaman in the world than American Jack; he had been bred to his work from infancy, and had been off in his fishing dory almost as soon as he could walk. When he grew older, he shipped on a merchant-marine or whaler, and in those warlike times, when our large merchant-marine was compelled to rely pretty much on itself for protection each craft had to be well handled; all who were not were soon weeded out by a process of natural selection. It was a rough school, but it taught Jack to be both skilful [sic] and self-reliant; and he was all the better fitted to become a man of war's man.[23]

TR had an equally high regard for the American officer corps. While a general admirer of the Royal Navy, he concluded that it had declined from "the commoner's service" through time to become a depository of second sons of landed peers. By the beginning of hostilities with the United States, the average British officer had become too complacent from too many victories and too little competition. In contrast, the American officer was at the height of his professional achievement:

> He had extricated himself by his own prowess or skill from the dangers of battle or storm; he owed his rank to the fact that he had proved worthy of it.

Thrown upon his own resources, he had learned self-reliance; he was a first-rate practical seaman, and prided himself on the way his vessel was handled. Having reached his rank by hard work, and knowing what real fighting meant, he was careful to see that his men were trained in the essentials of discipline, and that they knew how to handle guns in battle.[24]

These and other statements established Theodore Roosevelt as an authority on the connection between national character and sea power. His argument was clear and his logic clean and well supported. His work actually surpassed Mahan's later writings in terms of powerful exposition and brevity.

The 23-year-old politician from New York was even more emphatic with regard to the influence of government on sea power. *The Naval War of 1812* is replete with derogatory references to the American government of the early nineteenth century. In fact, only the judicial branch escapes his withering fire. He blasts Congress for failing to fund construction before the war of line-of-battle ships. TR concluded that "the only activity ever exhibited by Congress in materially increasing the navy previous to the war, had been in partially carrying out President Jefferson's ideas of having an enormous force of very worthless gunboats."[25]

When reviewing Roosevelt's opinions on the character of the American government, it is worth noting that he continued to express these views in later books. In the years following the tragic death of his first wife, Alice, Roosevelt retreated to the Dakotas to heal, pursue ranching, and write. In two biographies, *Thomas Hart Benton* (1887) and *Gouverneur Morris* (1888), Roosevelt used the careers of these early statesmen as a platform to expound on the failings of the early Congress in relation to sea power.

In praising Gouverneur Morris, a revolutionary leader, diplomat, and senator, Roosevelt castigated the Jefferson administration: "He (Morris) never showed greater wisdom than in his views about our navy; and his party, the Federalists, started to give us one; but it had hardly begun before the Jeffersonians came into power, and, with singular foolishness, stopped the work."[26]

The antinaval inclination of Jefferson's Democratic-Republicans found continued expression in the follow-on Jacksonian Democrats. Senator Thomas Hart Benton of Missouri, a devoted supporter of Andrew Jackson, espoused a philosophy that strongly influenced our national efforts for most of the nineteenth century. Roosevelt wrote that "Benton's opposition to [the Navy's] increase seems to have proceeded partly from bitter partisanship, partly from sheer ignorance, and partly from the doctrinaire dread of any kind of standing military or naval force, which he had inherited, with a good many similar ideas, from Jeffersonians."[27] Fresh memories of the tyranny of the strong central British government continued to haunt the nation for years to come.

Theodore Roosevelt held strong views about Thomas Jefferson. The nation's twenty-sixth president belittled its third president for following a policy of avoiding confrontation on the high seas and building gunboats capable only of coastal defense. While acknowledging Mr. Jefferson as "a man whose views and theories had a profound influence upon our national life," Roosevelt characterized him as "perhaps the most incapable executive that ever filled the presidential chair." James Madison, Jefferson's apprentice and political heir, fares only slightly better. According to TR, the Madison administration "drifted into a war which it had neither the wisdom to avoid nor the forethought to prepare for."[28] In his summation, Roosevelt found the federal government of that era unworthy of the American people and damaging to the nation's maritime destiny.

PROPHET OF PREPAREDNESS

Had Roosevelt written *The Naval War of 1812* and not another word on naval power, the work would have stood as a lasting achievement, but the author would have faded into obscurity. Theodore Roosevelt's prominence in our nation's history stands as a testament to his ability to combine unique personal strengths with a vision of national greatness. As a junior legislator in New York, TR demonstrated self-confidence and assurance in his own beliefs and values that is rarely found in someone so young. His books and correspondence from this early period reveal a man driven to realize a destiny, a destiny intertwined with public service. TR decided not to become a naturalist, a youthful fantasy, or join the family's glassworks business, but instead to pursue a career in government.

A central theme ran through his letters, articles, and books: the nation needed not only to build but to employ a modern fleet if it was to take its place on the world stage as a great power. This understanding set TR apart from Mahan, the thinker, and enabled the President to far exceed the naval officer's influence in the development of American naval power.

Preparedness became Roosevelt's touchstone throughout his tenure as Assistant Secretary of the Navy and then as Commander in Chief. This belief in preparedness led him as Assistant Secretary of the Navy in 1898 to send a telegram to Commodore George Dewey in China to coal his ships and be prepared for war with Spain. The need to ready American naval forces for battle on the open sea also partly inspired President Roosevelt to dispatch the Great White Fleet on its round-the-world cruise in 1907. From young historian to elder statesman, TR always stressed the requirement for the United States to maintain a strong Navy, and to be prepared to use it in support of national interests.

Roosevelt rarely missed an opportunity in his writings to castigate past administrations for failing to fund maintenance of a strong navy, resulting in greater cost and injury to the nation. He observed that "five years of war would involve more national expense than the support of a navy for twenty years, and until we rendered ourselves respectable, we should continue to be insulted."[29] In his *Thomas Hart Benton*, Roosevelt stated that in the 1820s the nation was, "as always, in our chronic state of utter defenselessness." He added, "our danger is always that we shall spend too little, and not too much, in keeping ourselves prepared for foreign war."[30] Roosevelt wrote passionately about the Jefferson administration's "miserable" gunboats: "The failure of the gunboats ought to have taught the lesson (though it did not) that too great economy in providing the means of defense may prove very expensive in the end, and that good officers and men are powerless when embarked in worthless vessels."[31]

TR preferred a navy of modern, powerful warships, even though few in number, as during the War of 1812, to a large fleet of obsolete vessels:

> Our navy in 1812 was the exact reverse of what our navy is now, in 1882. . . . We now have a large number of worthless vessels, standing very low down in their respective classes. We then possessed a few vessels, each unsurpassed by any foreign ship of her class. To bring up our navy to the condition in which it stood in 1812 it would not be necessary (although in reality both very wise and very economical) to spend any more money than at present; only instead of using it to patch up a hundred antiquated hulks, it should be employed in building half a dozen ships on the most effective model.[32]

In a sarcastic jab at the current administration, he drove home his point: "It is too much to hope that our political short-sightedness will ever enable us to have a navy that is first-class in point of size; but there certainly seems no reason why what ships we have should not be of the very best quality."[33] Roosevelt's passionate advocacy for a new, powerful fleet did not go unnoticed in political circles, and indeed later helped earn him an appointment as Assistant Secretary of the Navy.

Years before Mahan's seminal book reached the public, Theodore Roosevelt's writings and public actions demonstrated a clear understanding of sea power, and its importance to national defense and international greatness. At least one other naval strategist recognized TR's intellectual gifts. Rear Admiral Stephen B. Luce, who founded the Naval War College at Newport, Rhode Island, in 1884, made Roosevelt's *The Naval War of 1812* required reading for his student officers. Luce also served as host when Roosevelt delivered an address at the war college entitled "True Conditions of the War of 1812." The future president met Alfred Thayer Mahan during this all-important visit.

With the publication of Mahan's *The Influence of Sea Power Upon History*, Roosevelt knew that he had found a kindred spirit. After devouring the new book, TR wrote to Mahan: "During the last two days I have spent half my time, busy as I am, in reading your book. . . . I can say with perfect sincerity that I think it very much the clearest and most instructive general work of the kind with which I am acquainted. . . . I am greatly in error if it does not become a naval classic."[34]

Shortly afterward, TR published a review of Mahan's work in the noted literary journal, the *Atlantic Monthly*, in which he observed:

> He never for a moment loses sight of the relations which the struggles by sea bore to history of the time; and for the period which he covers, he shows, as no other writer has done, the exact points and the wonderful extent of the influence of the sea power of the various contending nations upon their ultimate triumph or failure, and upon the futures of the mighty races to which they belonged.[35]

Roosevelt repeatedly expressed his acceptance of Mahan's ideas in the years that followed, as he was again and again called upon to review the naval officer's books. In a typical critique, Roosevelt penned the following: "He did—what is so very rare—something absolutely original: he wrote with a philosophic comprehension of naval history in its relation to history generally such as no one else has shown."[36]

Mahan had no greater admirer than Theodore Roosevelt. In following years, Mahan's words appeared over and over in TR's speeches and writings. But Roosevelt had long before reached his own conclusions about the nature of sea power and its relationship to national strength and the international balance of power. These two towering American leaders, and their ideas about sea power and the state, would chart a new course for the United States and its Navy in the momentous twentieth century.

NOTES

1. Julius W. Pratt, *A History of United States Foreign Policy* (Englewood Cliffs, NJ: Prentice-Hall, 1955), 32.
2. W. D. Puleston, *Mahan: The Life and Work of Captain Alfred Thayer Mahan* (New Haven, CT: Yale University Press, 1939), 93.
3. Alfred T. Mahan, *The Influence of Sea Power Upon History, 1660–1783* (New York: Hill and Wang, 1957), 25.
4. Theodore Roosevelt, *Theodore Roosevelt: An Autobiography* (New York: Charles Scribner's Sons, 1926), 3.

5. Ibid., 14–15.

6. Ibid.

7. Ibid., 13.

8. Edmund Morris, *The Rise of Theodore Roosevelt* (New York: Coward, Mc-Cann and Geoghegan, Inc., 1979), 43.

9. F. C. Iglehart, *Theodore Roosevelt: The Man As I Knew Him* (New York: Charles Scribner's Sons, 1919), 121–22.

10. Roosevelt, *Autobiography*, 18.

11. Elting E. Morison, ed., *The Letters of Theodore Roosevelt,* vol. 1 (Cambridge, MA: Harvard University Press, 1951), 50.

12. Ibid., 52.

13. Roosevelt, *Autobiography*, 24.

14. Owen Wister, *Roosevelt: The Story of a Friendship* (New York: The Macmillan Co., 1930), 24.

15. Theodore Roosevelt, *The Naval War of 1812* (Annapolis: Naval Institute Press, 1987), 330–31.

16. Ibid., 165–66.

17. Ibid., 143.

18. Ibid., 394.

19. Ibid., 162–63.

20. Ibid., 290.

21. Mahan, *The Influence of Sea Power Upon History,* 39.

22. Roosevelt, *The Naval War of 1812,* 53.

23. Ibid., 52–53.

24. Ibid., 51–52.

25. Ibid., 397.

26. Ibid., 423.

27. Theodore Roosevelt, *The Works of Theodore Roosevelt, The National Edition,* vol. VII: *Thomas Hart Benton—Governeur Morris* (New York: Charles Scribner's Sons, 1926), 174–75.

28. Roosevelt, *The Naval War of 1812,* 405–6.

29. Ibid., 423.

30. Roosevelt, *Thomas Hart Benton—Governeur Morris,* 94.

31. Roosevelt, *The Naval War of 1812,* 210.

32. Ibid., 143–44.

33. Ibid.

34. Morison, *The Letters of Theodore Roosevelt,* vol. 1, 222.

35. Theodore Roosevelt, *The Works of Theodore Roosevelt, The National Edition,* vol. XII, *Literary Essays: The Influence of Sea Power* (New York: Charles Scribner's Sons, 1926), 266–67.

36. Ibid., 274.

SEVEN

THE EXPERIENCE OF THE SPANISH-AMERICAN WAR AND ITS IMPACT ON PROFESSIONAL NAVAL THOUGHT[1]

JOHN B. HATTENDORF

IT IS A COMMON-PLACE ASSUMPTION AMONG CRITICS of the armed forces that rigid military minds tend to prepare for the last war rather than to think inventively about the future. There is a worthwhile point in that thought, yet even the most advanced approaches of our own day do not permit us to know with any certainty what the future will bring. Taken to its extremes, focus on the future becomes mere speculation, unfounded by reality. In history, wars are common, but not continuous. Within the span of an individual's career in the military, it might occur perhaps once or twice, if at all. Thus, the study of the past is an important part of professional military and naval thinking, although academic historians always need to remind those in uniform that the value of historical study is found in terms of education and in broadening the basis for insight and analysis rather than in creating recipes for specific actions. The broad use of history in professional military education is part of a broader approach that includes understanding of current technological capabilities with reasoned speculation about the future, based on past performance and general understanding of the character, role, and limitations of armed force in society and in relations among nations.

Within this broad context, then, we find American naval officers, in the months and years prior to and just following the Spanish-American War, talking to each other in the world of professional debate on familiar subjects of the latest concern. In 1898, it had been more than 30 years since Americans had seen war at sea. The Civil War was the most recent experience of naval warfare for most Americans, and one had to look back a century to the Napoleonic wars to find practical examples of naval warfare on a global scale. Therefore, it is not surprising that the first theorists of naval warfare, working in the maelstrom of late-nineteenth-century technological change, first looked to the series of European wars between 1660 and 1815 for the foundation of their understanding. The initial historical studies of such pioneer British and American naval thinkers as John Knox Laughton, Philip Colomb, Alfred Thayer Mahan, and Julian Corbett all shared this predilection.

The founding of the U.S. Naval Institute at Annapolis in 1873, with its journal *Proceedings,* and the establishment of the Naval War College at Newport, Rhode Island, just over a decade later in 1884, mark the beginnings of the professionalization and the institutionalization of new approaches to naval thought in America. The most famous, and perhaps overemphasized, aspect of this development was Alfred Thayer Mahan's publication in 1890 of his Naval War College lectures under the well-remembered title, *The Influence of Sea Power Upon History, 1660–1783.* Yet, Mahan's historical lectures were only part of what the Naval War College was about. At the same time as they listened to Mahan, its students used the new methodology of war-gaming to examine and to evaluate the capabilities of developing naval technologies, while also looking at the broad structure of international relations and the growth of restraints on the use of force through international law.[2]

In 1898, professional thinking in the U.S. Navy encompassed much more than Mahan's work. Even in the area of historical study, James R. Soley had begun as early as 1884 to collect the operational records of the Civil War for publication and professional study. In supporting this work, Secretary of the Navy William C. Whitney declared in 1888:

> The Civil War is not only the first war in which naval operations on a great scale have been conducted since the introduction of steam, but it is the only war in which those modern appliances have been used which have revolutionized the art of naval warfare. The maintenance of steam blockade and the employment of commerce destroying steam cruisers, two of the most important operations of modern war, occurred only in this conflict.[3]

In 1894, the first volume of this series of naval documents appeared and, in May 1898, just as the battle of Manila Bay was being fought, volume seven was being printed at the Government Printing Office. These documentary volumes played an important role in contemporary professional naval thought in the 1890s, complementing the already clear idea that an understanding of the experience of the Civil War was key to preparation for future warfare. In delving into the professional thinking in the period leading up to the Spanish-American War, one can clearly see that influence, and one needs to be aware of it as a bench mark upon which new thought was occurring.

CONTINGENCY PLANNING

The first serious consideration of a possible naval war with Spain occurred as early as 1894 at the Naval War College. In that year, just ten years after the institution's founding, the president of the college, Captain Henry C. Taylor, had just initiated a new curriculum. Through it, the Naval War College planned to educate student officers by studying history as well as using war games to examine hypothetical and potential war situations. With faculty guidance and information from the Office of Naval Intelligence, Taylor believed that Naval War College students could function as a naval staff, demonstrating the way that a naval general staff could work, and eventually grow into a permanent fixture within the Navy. In particular, Taylor and others at the Naval War College were promoting the idea that naval operations could be much more successful if they were proceeded by planning, detailed preparation, and rational analysis of issues during peacetime, coupled with rapid execution of those plans in the event of war.

As part of the Naval War College's academic program in 1894, Taylor assigned three officer students in the class to develop a "Strategy in the Event of War with Spain." These students considered two different scenarios. The first one involved a war in which the United States was allied with France against Britain allied with Spain. The other scenario considered the United States fighting Spain alone. The following year, Taylor directed the class of 1895 to consider two situations: a general problem devoted to the defense of New England against Britain, and a special problem devoted to war between the United States and Spain. After the 1895 class had finished its work, the college faculty refined the students' efforts, developing a more advanced study that considered three alternative options for war with Spain: 1) a direct attack on Spain; 2) an attack on Spain's Pacific Ocean possessions, the Philippines and Guam; or 3) an attack on Spain's American colonies, Cuba and Puerto Rico. The college concluded that operations in the Pacific "would require fewer men and less money, and the issue of a resolute campaign against the Philippines might be regarded as reasonably certain to be successful."[4]

These early ideas about a war with Spain were forwarded to Washington and may have had some influence, but the next major step came when Lieutenant William W. Kimball, an officer from the Office of Naval Intelligence stationed at the Naval War College, prepared a study that envisaged a purely naval war based upon a blockade of Cuba. This approach would allow the Cubans to establish their own independent nation while avoiding an American invasion and preventing Spanish military interference. With this, Kimball considered two secondary campaigns. One was designed to hold the Spanish fleet in home waters by an American naval attack of Spanish coastal cities and coastal trade. The other campaign was an attack on the Philippines. Kimball's description of it reads like a description of eighteenth-century naval warfare. The United States could pursue this course

> for the purpose of reducing and holding Manila, of harassing trade, of cutting off revenue (especially that due to sugar and tobacco) from Spain, of occupying or at least blockading the Philippines principal ports so that the release of our hold on them may be used as an inducement to Spain to make peace after the liberation of Cuba.[5]

Kimball continued:

> The ease with which the revenue of the island could at once be attained and the fact that these revenues might be held until a war indemnity were satisfactorily arranged for, both indicate that Manila should be made a serious objective.[6]

The Naval War College considered Kimball's plan during the 1896 summer course. Much influenced by studying the U.S. Navy's experience in blockade operations during the American Civil War, as well as by Mahan's recent writings, the college criticized Kimball's plan, arguing that while the Philippine operations could be useful, the blockade of Cuba could not be effective until the Spanish fleet had been defeated. The reviewers added that operations in Spanish home waters should be carefully avoided until after the Cuban operations were completed. Reexamining the issue of a Manila campaign, the college concluded that an attack on Spain's Far Eastern possessions would not be profitable: "Success there, however, would not be of great value to us, as it would certainly not bring the enemy to terms."[7]

While the Naval War College reviewers found a sound purpose for operations in the Far East, they stressed that Cuban operations were the main issue of the war, and here blockade would play a major role. As Captain Caspar Goodrich of the Naval War College suggested, "the quicker this block-ade is established and the more efficient it is made the better; for judging by the experience of the Civil War, the army can hardly be expected to move for a month after the outbreak of the hostilities. Celerity on the part of the navy, might possibly, though not probably, render the army's cooperation unnecessary."[8]

Meanwhile, historical insight was used in another context. In Washing-ton, Congress had passed a joint resolution on April 6, 1896, calling for President Grover Cleveland to act more vigorously by recognizing the Cuban insurgency as a revolution and by offering direct American aid. While there was considerable support in Congress for such active interven-tion, several naval officers commented on the idea and debated whether or not, in the light of Wellington's experience in the Peninsular War, the United States could expect any substantial assistance from insurgent Cuban forces.[9]

In examining the possibility of a war with Spain in the years leading up to 1898, historical insights from both the Napoleonic wars and the Ameri-can Civil War can be found in some important areas of naval thinking. Like those earlier wars, the Spanish-American War created its own body of naval experience and provided the food for thought that both altered and ex-panded upon earlier understanding. Believing in the importance of this war as new material for future naval thinking, the Navy published nearly all the official operational reports of the war. On December 1, 1898, the Bureau of Navigation submitted a 700-page volume of documents that was collected, arranged, and edited by Ensign Herbert H. Ward as a full, volume-length appendix to *The Annual Report of the Secretary of the Navy.* It was later in-cluded in the President's Message to Congress.[10] This volume provided the essential raw material that established an immediate and authoritative basis for future reflections on the war.

One of the first, and probably the most famous and widely read, com-mentaries on the naval side of the war was Captain Mahan's *Lessons of the War with Spain,* which first appeared as a series of articles in the *Times* of London and in *McClure's* magazine between December 1898 and April 1899. It was then published separately as a book, and subsequently trans-lated into Dutch, French, German, Italian, and Spanish.[11] Reflecting Mahan's fundamental purpose in writing and teaching,[12] his series of arti-cles illustrated not only the unique aspects of the war, but "some of the el-ementary conceptions of warfare in general and of naval warfare in particular."[13] In writing these essays for the general public, Mahan believed that he could help create more public interest for military preparedness, thus indirectly inducing Congress to provide for the Army and Navy dur-ing periods of peace, as a means of averting warfare in the future. Addi-tionally, he thought that his exposition of the issues of naval conflict would help to educate the general public about war and enable them to avoid panic should the country have to face another war in the future.

In terms of the immediate political consequences of the war, it is interesting to us, a century later, to see that Mahan saw its most important consequences in Asia. He pointed out that, in his view, the most important factor was the appearance of American naval power in the Philippines, suddenly confronting "the quiet, superficially peaceful progress with which Russia was successfully advancing her boundaries in Asia, adding gain to gain, unrestrained and apparently irrestrainable."[14] Mahan underscored the point that the creation of an American presence in the Philippines was made possible through the friendliness of Great Britain in providing direct support for American naval preparations in Hong Kong. In Mahan's view, this encouragement from the major power of the day was paralleled by the growing perception in Japan and in Western nations of the critical importance of political issues in China for both trade and future economic development, and the potential value of an American presence in the solution of those problems.

In discussing the direct lessons of the Spanish-American War, Mahan was characteristically oblique in his approach, avoiding clear-cut conclusions and expressing his ideas through extended discourse surrounding detailed incidents. Among other things, he pointed out that if the United States had been more fully prepared militarily, Americans would have avoided the panic that swept the East Coast when the population imagined that the Spanish fleet might suddenly bombard New England ports.[15] With a similar approach, he drew attention to a wide-ranging collection of issues raised in the war. Among the variety were such key issues as the military importance of Puerto Rico to the safety of the future Panama Canal, the security of the sea lanes through the Caribbean, and their relationship to stability in Cuba.[16]

Another issue was the size and characteristics of warships, a question that had been raised even before the war. Given the fact that a certain number of dollars would build a certain number of tons, the question was a matter of deciding whether the investment should be made in a fewer number of larger ships, or a larger number of smaller ships. In approaching this issue, Mahan argued that there were two main considerations. First, he saw an advantage to limiting the size of battleships. With the total firepower of the fleet remaining approximately the same, limiting the size of battleships gave the fleet a flexibility and an advantage that could increase its offensive power, he argued. The second controlling factor was the ability of ships to steam a certain distance before refueling. The experience of the Spanish-American War suggested to Mahan that ships of 10,000 to 12,000 tons displacement were the optimum size, giving the most favorable relationship in maximum firepower of guns carried to the range of a ship's operations.

The American Civil War had suggested the importance of monitors—low-built, heavily armed ships—for coastal defense in smooth waters. The U.S. Navy, like other navies around the world, had adopted John Ericsson's revolutionary ship design. In 1898, the U.S. Navy had some 26,000 tons devoted to comparatively recently built monitor-type ships. "Had the Spanish guns at Santiago kept our fleet at greater distance," Mahan wrote, "we should have lamented still more bitterly the policy which gave us sluggish monitors for mobile battleships."[17] Behind Mahan's thinking on this point was the understanding that the U.S. Navy needed to change its traditional thinking about the employment of warships. From the beginning of its history, the Navy had tended to employ its vessels singly and independently. In the future, Mahan believed, the Navy should operate its ships as a fleet, using its various combatants as complementary units within a larger tactical organization.

One of the principal lessons of the war, in Mahan's mind, was that the U.S. Navy had too few major warships and had to economize too much, limiting the naval service's wartime operations. The main problem, he argued, was that there was no reserve. Throughout the operations off Santiago, for example, the Navy Department had to consider that there was no battleship available in a home port that could replace another seriously damaged or lost in action. Other writers of the day criticized the Navy's operations off Cuba for its lack of aggressive action in the way that Farragut had "damned the torpedoes" and steamed full speed ahead at Mobile Bay. The more-than-adequate reason, Mahan explained, was that the country could not at that time, under the political considerations of the moment, afford to risk the loss or disablement of a single battleship. "If we lost ten thousand men, the country could replace them," Mahan declared; "if we lost a battleship, it could not be replaced."[18] The point was that everything in the war depended upon naval force. With every military operation taking place overseas, "a million of the best soldiers would have been powerless in the face of hostile control of the sea."[19]

FOREIGN REACTION TO THE WAR

Throughout his book, Mahan stressed specific issues that were important aspects in gaining public support for building and increasing the size of the American navy. In this, Mahan was merely reflecting a more widespread view. In an 1899 classified report read only by naval officers, the Office of Naval Intelligence circulated its analysis of the impact of the war on foreign navies. It reported that foreign navies had drawn similar conclusions about the war, although the staff intelligence officer who prepared the report cautioned that "these foreign views and tendencies are given as being worthy of consideration, but not as being necessarily applicable to our own service."[20] Certainly, the Spanish-American War loomed large in American minds and not everyone around the world was willing to see it in the same light. The U.S. Naval Attaché in London reported in 1899 that the Royal Navy seemed little interested in the war, since the professional aspects and the outcome were already known.[21] Colonel Charles Callwell of the British Army, the author of the now-classic study of joint operations, *Military Operations and Maritime Preponderance*, wrote in 1905: "Admiral Dewey's victory in Manila Bay, striking as it was, was over shore batteries that were out of date, over mines that did not go off, and over war-vessels in every way inferior to those of the attacking squadron: the enterprise turned out to be a far less difficult one than it appeared to be, and its merits lie rather in the fact of its having been attempted than in its actual execution."[22] Similarly, Rear Admiral Max Plüddemann, writing in *Marine-Rundschau* in November 1898, noted that "the events of the war just ended show nothing which might lead to a radical revolution of present ideas as to rational warfare and the use of modern war material."[23]

It may well be that some American naval officers exaggerated the impact of the experience in the Spanish-American War, tending, perhaps, to attribute the origins of contemporary long-term and worldwide naval developments to themselves. Nevertheless, professionals in other countries did study the war. Around the globe, the most striking tendency in the naval world was the marked effort of all major maritime powers to increase their naval strength and to consider development and growth. The origins of this growth can in no way be attributed to the Spanish-American War, but its experience certainly seemed to have some direct effect on foreign navies. The major naval powers, Britain, France, Italy, and most recently Germany, had already begun to build battleships and to consider them the main fighting strength of a navy. "This view was held long before the Spanish armored cruisers were destroyed at Santiago," the Office of Naval Intelligence reported, "but it now meets with general acceptance."[24] The experience of Santiago impressed on foreign observers the need for mobility with heavy guns. It underscored the need to build battleships that would have the best available protection and be faster, ideally capable of a minimum operational speed of 15 knots for tactical evolutions. Such standards rendered the vast majority of battleships obsolete and demanded the use of the latest developments in engineering. Prior to the war, some naval experts had claimed that armored cruisers were superior to battleships, but this claim died away after the destruction of the Spanish fleet.

Among other types of vessels, the war discredited further construction of heavily armed coastal vessels, such as the monitor-type. There were several reasons for this. First of all, naval officers foresaw that future conflicts would involve offensive actions at sea against similar vessels, rather than defensive combat in protected coastal waters. As Russian Admiral Stepan Makarov put it, "in a naval battle it is better to rely upon the strength of the weapon rather than upon the solidity of the shield."[25] The large European navies concluded that coastal defense could be carried out by the older designs of battleships as they came out of fleet service. Fast cruisers remained important types of vessels. With speed and endurance, they were the modern "eyes of the fleet," as fast frigates had been in the days of Nelson. Reflections on the war were particularly important to a change that led to development of the small torpedo boat into the larger, more heavily armed destroyer-type vessel. While small, highly maneuverable torpedo boats were earlier thought to have been a possible deadly threat to battleships, the Spanish-American War lent no encouragement to this view, giving further weight to the general tendency to disregard them. No use was made of submarines in the war, and several countries were just beginning to explore this type of vessel.

One of the major results of the war was an emphasis on gunnery. Many observers concluded that rapid-fire guns of a moderate caliber were the best type to employ in the future. In the light of this observation, German officials were said to have reduced the maximum size of the heaviest guns on their new battleships to a caliber of 9.45 inches, while the Royal Navy laid new stress on its 6-inch guns. In other areas of gunnery, the war gave impetus to the further use of metal cartridge casings, improved mechanical means to supply ammunition to guns, and the improvement of smokeless powder that had fewer noxious effects on gun crews.

The war brought out, in particular, a humanitarian desire to improve the conditions under which seamen operated and fought their ships. This was a key factor in a new emphasis on increasing the armor protection of battleships. Professional observers quickly saw that the unarmored portions of Spanish warships had merely helped to explode small caliber ammunition and kill and demoralize ships' crews. This conclusion dramatically reinforced earlier and similar observations from the Sino-Japanese War. As an American intelligence officer put it, "the appalling disablement of crew which, under well-directed fire, may occur on board armored ships lacking widely distributed protection is now fully appreciated."[26]

In a related development, the way in which American gunfire had started fires, leading to the destruction and abandonment of the Spanish ships, inspired an immediate move to abolish wooden furniture and decorative wooden paneling in future warship design and construction. American naval officers had already been aware of the potential dangers posed by these materials on board modern warships. Sigsbee had commented on them when he had visited Spanish warships before the war in January 1898, and, most famously, Dewey had dramatically removed the wooden furniture and paneling from his ships before the action at Manila Bay. Nevertheless, the example of the fires on board Spanish ships provided practical experience to back up a theoretical point. As the Office of Naval Intelligence reported shortly after the war, other navies took the same point to heart: "In some of the latest ships the furniture is of metal or of fire-proofed wood, the steel bulkheads have ornamental asbestos covering, and the steel decks are given a plastic nonflammable coating."[27] In addition to providing further impetus to discontinue the use of wooden furniture and wooden ships, the experience of the war also hastened the rise of measures to increase fire-fighting capabilities on board ship. Spurring this effort was the knowledge that the crew of at least one Spanish cruiser at Santiago had failed to lay out fire hoses in preparation for action. When American shells caused fires, the Spaniard had no readily available means of fighting them.

While both official pronouncements and the popular press made much of the fact that the U.S. Navy's gunnery had been so effective that it totally destroyed two Spanish squadrons, both American[28] and foreign gunnery specialists saw that it was really very poor. As early as June 1899, Lieutenant John M. Ellicott published an article on the effect of gunfire at the Battle of Manila Bay. While the main thrust of his remarks was that modern ships were liable to be placed out of action by fires and personnel casualties before they were sunk by gunfire, he included data that showed that the Spanish squadron was destroyed by less that 141 hits. Other sources showed that, although the American gunnery was superior to that of the Spanish, it was slow and very inaccurate. A British officer viewing the wrecked Spanish ships a month after the battle reported home:

> The only conclusion that could be drawn . . . is that the ships under Admiral Montojo were indifferently fought and that he and his commanding officers were too ready to run their ships on shore, scuttle them and burn them while the crews deserted to the beach.[29]

While a widespread legend developed about the effectiveness of American gunnery that served to spur the movement in Britain to support improved gunnery, gunnery experts knew that it was not true and that much improvement was necessary.[30] Not long afterwards, in 1901, Lieutenant William S. Sims of the U.S. Navy expressed his awareness of this situation, while serving on the Asiatic Station, when he observed the far superior gunnery of HMS *Terrible,* commanded by Captain Percy Scott.[31] This was the beginning point from which Sims, through the personal patronage of Theodore Roosevelt, came to lead the dramatic improvements in American naval gunnery, paralleling those of Scott in the Royal Navy.[32]

In 1899, the flamboyant Captain Bowman McCalla, winner of two Medals of Honor during the war, lectured at the Naval War College on his own "Lessons of the Late War."[33] As the commanding officer of the USS *Marblehead* at the blockade of Cienfuegos and the officer who led the attack that captured Guantánamo Bay, his views tended to focus at the tactical level. He noted such technical things as marine growth preventing Spanish mines from exploding, the need to enforce strict quarantine and health regulations in the fleet to prevent tropical diseases (particularly yellow fever) from disabling the fleet, and the total lack of any discipline in gunfire control in both the Army and Navy. In the last regard, he recounted the strange incident of how his own ship had accidentally been taken under fire when a lookout on another American combatant had mistaken the sudden appearance of a railroad train traveling along the beach as an attacking torpedo boat! On a quite different level, he noted the need to control waste and refuse from ships in order to conceal the movements of ships. After capturing Guantánamo, McCalla learned to his disgust that one of the most popular duty posts for Spanish sentries was one where they could forage for the food and refuse thrown as waste from the American ships offshore.

More importantly, he noted that there had been little opportunity to apply fleet or squadron tactics against enemy ships or shore batteries, but, in his opinion, there was a prevailing and unhealthy tendency in the Navy to think that "the fewest and the simplest movements are all that are required."[34] Here, he raised a highly technical subject that he dealt with in detail in other lectures and papers. Turning to other issues in his broad summary of the lessons of the war, McCalla was particularly critical of the sinking of the coal ship *Merrimac* in the entrance to Santiago harbor. Although not wanting to impugn the heroism of his comrades, he still made his point clear: "Under such circumstances success was not probable, but as the attempt failed and did not prevent Cervera from coming out to meet defeat, we can never regret that the *Merrimac* was sent in, for it gave the Navy an opportunity of exhibiting such splendid gallantry and fearlessness of death that every American must be proud of Hobson and his companions."[35]

McCalla's final points touched on such broad issues as logistical support, strategic direction of the war, the broad relationship between coastal defense and naval operations, and national military preparedness. With devastating criticism, McCalla declared

although it has been stated in the newspapers and generally believed by the public that the navy was prepared for war, the truth is that we were only less unprepared than Spain. We were practically unprovided with smokeless powder for the guns, our coal was inferior, there was no reserve ammunition and we were without fresh-water boats. There were no colliers, supply ships, float-ing machine-shops, nor ambulance ships; and most important of all, there was no reserve of personnel for our under-manned ships, all of our cruisers and battleships being in commission, with two or three exceptions. The naval base at Key West was entirely unprovided with the plant required to supply the needs of the fleet.[36]

INTERNATIONAL LAW

One of the operational issues that McCalla had discussed in detail was the U.S. Navy's attempts to cut the telegraph cables between Cuba and Madrid.[37] Dewey had undertaken similar operations at Manila. These oper-ations raised a new feature in naval warfare and the issue was widely dis-cussed both before and after the war as an aspect of what today might be called "information warfare." Vice Admiral Sir Philip Colomb, in the 1899 third edition of his influential book, *Naval Warfare,* added a 51-page ap-pendix analyzing the war, largely based on the U.S. Navy's published docu-ments of the war.[38] In his widely read analysis, he observed that the U.S. Navy depended on cable communication with Washington and raised the point that cutting cables was a matter that touched on international law.

At that point, the U.S. Navy had no formally established expert in the in-ternational law of naval warfare, although the topic had been taught at the Naval War College since its founding by visiting academics, such as profes-sors Thomas S. Woolsey of Yale, John Bassett Moore of Columbia, and George Grafton Wilson of Brown. The only naval officer who knew the sub-ject in depth was Commander Charles Stockton, who had developed a keen personal interest in the topic and had taken the time to teach himself.[39] In 1894, he volunteered to prepare the international law lectures of Harvard's Professor Freeman Snow for the U.S. Navy's first manual of international law.[40] In 1898, Stockton found himself appointed as the President of the Naval War College, when the students and all the rest of the staff were sent off to sea for the duration of the Spanish-American War. During this period, the Navy Department ordered him to obtain the most up-to-date informa-tion from each of the Navy's fleet commanders at sea, including George Dewey and William T. Sampson, and to revise and enlarge the manual of in-ternational law. The war had shown that such material was urgently needed in the fleet. Completing this work in October 1898, Stockton sent the man-uscript to Washington for publication by the Government Printing Office.[41] Among the issues that he covered, which had been raised by new experience in the war, were blockade operations, neutrality, the capture of private prop-erty at sea, privateering, customs administration of captured ports, and the termination of war.[42]

As president of the college in 1899, he invited Captain McCalla to give his critique of American operations in the war with Spain. But Stockton made sure that both naval history and international law were related to the operational analysis. Representative of a trend in the professional military discussions of the day, Stockton lectured on a historical subject raised by the war. He described the history of English joint operations directed against Puerto Rico and Cuba in the sixteenth through the eighteenth centuries, pointing out some modern parallels to historical experience. In addition, he gave a lecture on the legal aspects of "Submarine Telegraph Cables in Wartime."[43] He concluded that overseas "cable communication generally should . . . be kept open for commercial or other innocent intercourse, and in many cases government censorship can meet the circumstances and requirements of the war and prevent injury to a belligerent."[44] This was only one point among many detailed questions relating to international law that arose during the war.

Shortly after the academic course ended at the Naval War College in October 1899, the Judge Advocate General of the Navy forwarded to Stockton for comment an unofficial letter to the Secretary of the Navy from Lieutenant Commander William W. Kimball. The latter suggested that the Navy Department issue an authoritative and mandatory code or manual to cover all cases of international law that might occur in the experience of a naval officer. While Stockton agreed with Kimball's suggestion that it would be desirable to provide officers with such a manual, he had considerable doubt about the practicality of doing so. "International Law is a plant of slow growth," he wrote, "and its usages must be commonly and internationally accepted. Precedents from our departments are materials for future rules rather than present ones and it is worse than useless to promulgate as rules anything which is not regarded and accepted as such by other nations."[45] While Stockton found most of Kimball's suggestions impractical, he seized on one point, "the preparation of regulations upon the laws and usage of war upon the sea."[46] He observed that Dr. Francis Lieber had prepared instructions during the Civil War for the U.S. Army to regulate land warfare. Stockton noted that they had been "epoch making and redounded greatly to the credit of the author, the war department and the country."[47] Although designed as regulations for the U.S. Army alone, the regulations had become the model for similar codes in other countries. Moreover, in 1880 the Institute of International Law used them as the basis to formulate a code of the law of war on land for universal use. The Navy had nothing as comprehensive, although a set of French 1870 instructions and the U.S. Navy's General Order 492 of 1898 dealt with some of the pertinent issues. The time was ripe to remedy the situation. "The results of the 1899 Hague Conference give new matter for such a code of instructions," Stockton wrote. He added:

Now that we are at peace with the outside world the time would be an excellent one to draw up in accordance with the advanced humanity of the times, a code that would lead the world. As these instructions would not require any international action, and are directed to our own service, they would be undisputed authority, providing always they are in accord with definitely established international law and usage and the dictates of humanity.[48]

Within a week after sending this letter, Stockton received in reply orders from Secretary of the Navy John D. Long, dated November 2, 1899, directing him to prepare a draft comprehensive code, elaborating on the legal conventions established in the recent Hague Conference and embodying the laws of war at sea. Completing the code by the following May, Long issued it to the U.S. Navy in a 27-page pamphlet on June 27, 1900, in General Order 551, it "having been approved by the President of the United States."[49] Within a year, the code began to be favorably noticed overseas. The Naval Correspondent of the *Times* of London wrote, "this little Code of Laws deserves to be noted as another product of the United States Naval War College, to which we owe Captain Mahan's work on sea power."[50] In this case, however, it was a direct result of the experience of the U.S. Navy in the Spanish-American War. While the code remained in force for the U.S. Navy only until 1904, it remained the model for international negotiations at the London Conference in 1908 and 1909 and continues to be an important precedent for the current development of the law of naval warfare.

NAVAL ADMINISTRATION

In terms of future American naval development and finding solutions to the many issues that the experience of the war raised in the minds of professional naval officers, naval administration was a particular concern. For naval reformers in the 1880s, one of the central problems of the Civil War had been the Navy's difficulty managing the various naval bureau chiefs while, at the same time, conducting a war. Even in 1885, Secretary of the Navy William Whitney had reported to Congress that the separate executive responsibilities of the bureau chiefs made it impossible for them to provide him with military guidance on the art and conduct of war at sea. From this point, one can date a 30-year professional debate centering on the role and function of a professional naval chief in relation to the bureau chiefs and the secretary of the navy. After a massive outpouring of articles, reports, and discussions, and several experiments, in 1915 the Navy established the Office of the Chief of Naval Operations. This marked the beginning of the Navy's modern permanent staff system employing uniformed officers.[51]

The movement to improve naval management had begun at the Naval War College in the 1880s and early 1890s and is associated in particular with two former presidents of that institution, Rear Admiral Stephen B. Luce and Rear Admiral Henry C. Taylor. Both strongly advocated creation of a general staff for the Navy, emulating aspects of the German General Staff system.

At the urging of Admiral Taylor, Secretary of the Navy Long created, at the outset of the war in 1898, a temporary naval war strategy board, which initially included Assistant Secretary of the Navy Theodore Roosevelt, Mahan, the Chief of the Bureau of Navigation, the Chief Intelligence Officer, and several others. The functions of this board were broadly those that Taylor foresaw for a permanent naval staff: preparing contingency plans, employing the fleet, and collating intelligence information. As Captain William L. Rodgers noted, it was "the only organization either in the War or Navy department that was unembarrassed by the pressing administrative details. It being ready and willing the President turned to it because nobody else was free to answer his demands."[52] Mahan, Luce, and others urged the Secretary of the Navy to perpetuate the Naval War Board, in the hope that it could evolve into the larger and permanent staff they wanted to see. Secretary Long, however, disestablished it immediately after the war. The fact of the Navy's prewar unpreparedness and the board's wartime work suggested that such a body was sorely needed. The Navy's bureau chiefs, however, stoutly resisted any organizational action that would limit their authority. Congress and the American public, despite the views of these professional officers, could see no reason to improve the Navy, which had just won a war.

Fortunately for the Navy's reform-minded officers, George Dewey's victory at Manila Bay cast him in the role of national hero and gave him a lifetime sinecure with the unique rank of "Admiral of the Navy." The Navy was unsure how to employ so senior and so prestigious an officer afterward, but its reformist officers found a solution that also furthered their own agenda. Taylor convinced Secretary Long to create the General Board of the Navy, and to assign Dewey as its permanent president. Long acceded in March 1900, but insisted that the board was "avowedly an experiment," and declared that he "would dissolve it the moment it was not useful."[53]

Dewey's 17 years in that post gave the board both prestige and longevity that it could not otherwise have achieved. Despite the conservative admiral's constant desire to steer a middle course in all controversies and to avoid taking radical positions,[54] Dewey headed a General Board that became the principal instrument for pursuing the technical development of the Navy. Time and again, the General Board heard arguments and made decisions for improvements on the basis of the Navy's experience and deficiencies discovered in the Spanish-American War. In 1906, as just one example, Mahan wrote a history of "The Work of the Naval War Board of 1898"[55] for the General Board to use in its further deliberations that proved useful in development of the naval staff.

In the years between the Spanish-American War and America's entry into World War I in 1917, the perceptions of American naval officers about their most recent wartime experience merged with their adoption of new technologies that created more powerful, better-armed, and better-equipped ships. For example, in 1905, Secretary of the Navy Charles Bonaparte ended consideration of Civil War–type monitors because he believed that "the lessons of recent warfare" showed them to be entirely outmoded.[56] Through the direction of the General Board, the Navy's ships were forged into fleets for multi-ship operations, and the naval service became truly professional in its administration.[57]

The Spanish-American War did not revolutionize thinking about the future of naval warfare, but it did solidify a number of existing trends and ideas. The professional officers of the U.S. Navy differed from foreign naval officers and the American public in their appreciation of the Spanish-American War. American naval officers were happy to receive the praise for their notable wartime victories. But they were also conscious of the Navy's serious limitations, which the war had revealed. Many of them believed that had they faced a more capable foe, the results might have been quite different. With the experience of 1898 behind them, the professional men of the early twentieth century were able to devise new administrative structures, methods of operation, training procedures, and doctrine that contributed to a broadly based direction of naval power.[58] The experience of the war reinforced in professional naval officers the will and the determination to eradicate those serious weaknesses that had existed in 1898 and to build a Navy that would be better prepared and stronger, should war occur again.

NOTES

1. This paper was first delivered on April 11, 1998, at the "A Splendid Little War and Its Aftermath" conference, sponsored by the Anne S. K. Brown Military Collection, Brown University, Providence, Rhode Island. The final version, delivered at the October 21, 1998, symposium "Theodore Roosevelt, the U.S. Navy, and the Spanish-American War" at the U.S. Navy Memorial in Washington, D.C., has benefited from the constructive criticism of participants at the Brown University conference as well as from Captain Frank Snyder, USN (Ret.) at the U.S. Naval War College, and Dr. Michael J. Crawford and Mark L. Hayes of the Early History Branch, Naval Historical Center.

2. For a description of the history of these developments, see John C. Hattendorf et al., *Sailors and Scholars: The Centennial History of the Naval War College* (Newport, RI: Naval War College Press, 1984), chap. 2.

3. *Annual Report of the Secretary of the Navy, 1888* quoted in "Introduction," *Official Records of the Union and Confederate Navies in the War of the Rebellion* (Washington: Government Printing Office, 1894), series I, vol. 1, vii.

4. Hattendorf et al., *Sailors and Scholars,* 45–46. See also David F. Trask, *The War with Spain in 1898* (New York: Macmillan, 1981), chap. 4; Ronald Spector, "Who Planned the Attack on Manila Bay?," *Mid-America* 53 (Apr 1971): 94–102; Ronald Spector, *Professor of War: The Naval War College and the Development of the Naval Profession* (Newport, RI: Naval War College Press, 1977), 89–95.

5. Naval War College, Naval Historical Collection: Record Group 8, Series I, Box 44.

6. Kimball, in *Loc. cit.,* Commander Bowman McCalla, "War With Spain," (1897), 2.

7. Kimball, in McCalla, "War With Spain," 2.

8. "Rough Draft of Official Plan (Jul 1897) in event of operations against Spain in Cuba, with suggestions by Captain C. F. Goodrich," 1.

9. Ibid., 3, and McCalla, "War With Spain," 2.

10. *A Message from the President of the United States to the Two Houses of Congress at the beginning of the Third Session of the Fifty-Fifth Congress with the Reports of the Heads of Departments and selections from Accompanying Documents* (Washington: Government Printing Office, 1899), vol. iv.

11. A. T. Mahan, *Lessons of the War with Spain and Other Articles* (Boston: Little, Brown & Co., 1899). For the publishing details of the other versions and translations, see Hattendorf and Hattendorf, comps., *A Bibliography of the Works of Alfred Thayer Mahan* (Newport, RI: Naval War College Press, 1986), items A7, D39, D41, D42, D44, D45, D51, E28, E31-E40, F18-F27.

12. For a general analysis of Mahan's thought that stresses the importance of these aspects, see Jon T. Sumida, *Inventing Grand Strategy and Teaching Command: The Classic Works of Alfred Thayer Mahan Reconsidered* (Baltimore: Johns Hopkins University Press, 1997).

13. Mahan, *Lessons,* v.

14. Ibid., vii.

15. Ibid., 17–19.

16. Ibid., 26–29.

17. Ibid., 53.

18. Ibid., 185–86.

19. Ibid.

20. Lieutenant Commander George H. Peters, "Recent Tendencies of Foreign Naval Development and the Effect thereon of the Recent War with Spain," in Office of Naval Intelligence, *Information from Abroad. Notes on Naval Progress, November 1899,* General Information Series, no. XII (Washington: Government Printing Office, 1899), 7–16, quote at 7.

21. National Archives, Record Group 45, Subject File 1775–1910, VN (Naval Policy), entry 464: Letter from Lieutenant Commander John C. Colwell, USN, September 16, 1899, quoted in Richard W. Peuser, "Documenting United States Naval Activities during the Spanish-American War," *Prologue* 30 (Apr 1998): 41.

22. Charles E. Callwell, *Military Operations and Maritime Preponderance: Their Relations and Interdependence.* With an introduction and notes by Colin S. Gray, Classics of Seapower series (Annapolis, MD: Naval Institute Press, 1996), 116.

23. M. Plüddemann, konteradmiral a. D., "Der Spanish-Nordamerikanische Krieg," *Marine-Rundschau* (1898), 904–14; "II: Bis zum 25. juni 1898," *Marine-Rundschau* (1898), 1078–94; and "III: Bis zum 12. augusti 1898," *Marine-Rundschau* (1898), 1225–52; partially translated and circulated in English to the U.S. Navy, first under the title Office of Naval Intelligence. *Information From Abroad. War Notes,* no. II. *Comments of Rear-Admiral Max Plüddemann, German Navy, on the Main Features of the War with Spain* (Washington: Government Printing Office, 1898) and then, later, printed in U.S. Naval Institute *Proceedings* 24 (1898): 771–88.

24. Peters, "Recent Tendencies," 7.

25. "Professional Notes: Russian Views of Our War," U.S. Naval Institute *Proceedings,* XIV (1898): 791.

26. Peters, "Recent Tendencies," 12.

27. Ibid., 12–13.

28. John M. Ellicott, "Effect of Gunfire, Battle of Manila Bay, 1 May 1898," U.S. Naval Institute *Proceedings* 25 (1899): 323–34.

29. Public Record Office, Kew, ADM 1/7371: Lieutenant Commander George A. Hardinge, RN, to Vice Admiral Sir Edward Seymour. Report of the Visit of HMS *Rattler* to the Philippines.

30. Arthur J. Marder, *The Anatomy of Seapower: A History of British Naval Policy in the Pre-Dreadnought Era, 1880–1905* (New York: Alfred Knopf, 1940), 387–88.

31. Admiral Sir Percy Scott, *Fifty Years in the Royal Navy* (New York: George H. Doran, 1919), 153–55.

32. See Elting E. Morison, *Admiral Sims and the Modern American Navy* (Boston: Houghton Mifflin, 1942), particularly chaps. 8, 9, and 15.

33. Naval War College Archives, Record Group 15, Box 1: Captain Bowman McCalla, "Lessons of the Spanish American War," 1899.

34. Ibid., 25.

35. Ibid., 33.

36. Ibid., 63.

37. Ibid., 44–54.

38. Vice Admiral P. H. Colomb, *Naval Warfare: Its Ruling Principles and Practice Historically Treated.* With an introduction by Barry M. Gough. Classics of Seapower series (Annapolis, MD: Naval Institute Press, 1990). Two volumes. In this definitive edition, the Spanish-American War appendix appears in vol. 2, chap. 20, 518–70.

39. For a detailed study of Stockton, see Hattendorf, "Rear Admiral Charles Stockton, The Naval War College, and the Law of Naval Warfare" in Leslie C. Green and Michael N. Schmitt, eds., *The Law of Armed Conflict: Into the Next Millennium*, International Law Studies, vol. 71 (Newport, RI: Naval War College Press, 1998), xvii-lxxii.

40. Charles H. Stockton, *International Law. Lectures Delivered at the Naval War College by Freeman Snow, Ph.D., LL.B., late Instructor in International Law in Harvard University. Prepared and Arranged for Publication by Charles H. Stockton* (Washington: Government Printing Office, 1895).

41. Charles H. Stockton, *A Manual Based Upon Lectures Delivered at the Naval War College by Freeman Snow, Ph.D., LL.B., late Instructor in International Law in Harvard University. (Second Edition.) Prepared and Arranged for Publication by the Direction of the Navy Department by Commander C.H. Stockton, U.S.N.* (Washington: Government Printing Office, 1898).

42. Ibid., 80, 82, 109, 113, 119, 174-79.

43. The manuscripts of all his 1899 lectures are in Naval War College Archives, Record Group 14: Faculty and Staff presentations, Box 1: 1886-1900. He later published revised versions of both lectures: Charles H. Stockton, "Submarine Cables in Time of War," U.S. Naval Institute *Proceedings* 14 (1898): 451-56, and "An Account of Some Past Military and Naval Operations Directed Against Porto Rico and Cuba," U.S. Naval Institute *Proceedings* 26 (1900): 457-75.

44. "Submarine Cables," U.S. Naval Institute *Proceedings* 14 (1898): 455.

45. Letter from Stockton to Judge Advocate General, 26 October 1899. Naval War College Archives, Record Group 1, Box 7. Letterbook 1897-1900, 314-18, quote at 314.

46. Ibid., 317.

47. Ibid.

48. Ibid., 317-18.

49. *Naval War Code* (1900).

50. "A Naval War Code," *Times* [of London], Apr 5, 1901.

51. Samuel P. Huntington, *The Soldier and the State* (New York: Belknap Press, 1957), 248.

52. William L. Rodgers, "The Relations of the War College to the Navy Department," U.S. Naval Institute *Proceedings* 38 (Sep 1912): 844, quoted in Commander Daniel J. Costello, USN, "Planning for War: A History of the General Board of the Navy, 1900-1914." Unpublished Ph.D. thesis, Tufts University, 1968, 17.

53. Quotations from U.S. Congress. House, Naval Affairs Committee. *Hearings on Appropriation Bill for 1905 Subjects and on H.R. 15043 for General Board.* 58th Congress, 2nd Session. House Report No. 164 (Washington: Government Printing Office, 1904), 951, quoted in Costello, "Planning for War," 22.

54. Ronald Spector, *Admiral of the New Empire: The Life and Career of George Dewey* (Columbia: University of South Carolina Press, 1988), 204.

55. "The Work of the Naval War Board, 1898," in Robert Seager II and Doris Maguire, eds., *Letters and Papers of Alfred Thayer Mahan* (Annapolis, MD: Naval Institute Press, 1975), vol. 3, 627–43.

56. *Annual Report of the Navy Department for the Year 1905* (Washington: Government Printing Office, 1906), 24, quoted in George W. Baer, *One Hundred Years of Sea Power: The U.S. Navy, 1890–1990* (Stanford: Stanford University Press, 1994), 32.

57. Costello, "Planning for War," 337.

58. For a discussion with further background to this point, see Hattendorf, "Technology and Strategy: A Study in the Professional Thought of the U.S. Navy, 1898–1917," in Hattendorf, *Naval History and Maritime Strategy: Collected Essays* (Malabar, FL: Robert Krieger Publishing, 2000), 29–57.

EIGHT

THE INFLUENCE OF THE SPANISH-AMERICAN WAR ON THE U.S. MARINE CORPS

JACK SHULIMSON

THE SPANISH-AMERICAN WAR PROVED TO BE THE CRUCIBLE for the U.S. Marine Corps. While not fully knowing how they would use it, soon after the war's outbreak naval authorities ordered establishment of a Marine battalion with its own transport. The activities of this battalion, whose men numbered less than a quarter of the active Marine Corps, not only received public approbation, but also suggested a change in the future relationship between the Marine Corps and the Navy.

Even after the sinking of the *Maine* in February 1898, the role of the Marine Corps in a war with Spain remained vague. In March, Secretary of the Navy John D. Long explained the need for more Marines in terms of their traditional ship-board and guard missions. The authoritative *Army and Navy Journal,* however, reported on March 12, 1898, that Marine Commandant Colonel Charles Heywood had orders to form two battalions ready to deploy on short notice. At the same time, an article appeared in the Naval Institute *Proceedings* proposing the establishment of fleet advance bases with a defensive ground force. The only obvious source to provide such protection for an advanced base was the Marine Corps.[1]

Lieutenant Colonel Robert Huntington, commander of the New York Barracks and the likely commander of any Marine expeditionary force, reflected upon the uncertainties of the Marine role and the questionable readiness of its aging officer corps. Coincidentally, on the same day as the sinking of the *Maine*, he wrote that most senior captains were "fit for service in barracks, but age has decreased . . . [their] power of resisting the hardship and exposure incident to service in the field."[2]

On March 30, 1898, with the possibility of war much closer, Huntington speculated that Colonel Heywood planned to send him "to Key West to guard a coal pile." He allowed, however, that "there is of course a possibility that we might go to Cuba. I cannot say I enjoy the prospect very much, but as . . . the war is one of humanity, I am willing to take the personal risk." Huntington proved right on both counts; he and his Marines later went to Key West and Cuba.[3]

By early April, the Navy had completed its initial preparations. On April 6, 1898, Secretary Long ordered Captain William T. Sampson, commander of the North Atlantic Squadron at Key West, to establish a blockade of Cuba after the outbreak of hostilities. Whether influenced by the unreadiness of the Army or as part of the general mobilization, Captain Sampson asked Secretary Long for the deployment of two battalions of Marines. On April 16, Colonel Heywood received verbal orders to make the necessary arrangements. By April 20, the Marines had assembled 450 men from various East Coast navy yards at the New York Barracks. The department had decided against a second battalion. Instead, the Marines strengthened the one battalion with another 200 men. The 1st Battalion of Marines, under the command of Huntington, then consisted of 631 enlisted men, 21 officers, and 1 Navy surgeon, organized into 5 infantry companies and 1 artillery company.[4]

On Friday, April 22, 1898, the newly purchased Navy transport *Panther* docked at the Brooklyn Navy Yard. By 2000, with the battalion embarked, the *Panther* set sail. The men on board were crowded and uncomfortable. The troops carried with them the equipment and supplies necessary to sustain them in the field. Items included mosquito netting, woolen and linen clothing, heavy and lightweight underwear, wheelbarrows, pick axes, shovels, barbed wire cutters, tents, and medical supplies. In addition, the artillery company took with it four 3-inch rapid-fire guns. Morale among the men and officers was high.[5]

The specific mission of the Marine battalion remained unclear. When the unit was formed, a staff officer wrote that the Marines "are to have no connection whatever with the army, and are to report, and be at the disposal of the Commander-in-Chief of the North Atlantic Fleet." Among the officers and men of the battalion, speculation about their objectives abounded.[6]

On the evening of April 23, the *Panther* arrived at Hampton Roads. Lieutenant Colonel Huntington received orders that the battalion would stay on board ship. With the arrival of cruiser *Montgomery* on the morning of April 26, the *Panther* steamed out of port. As the warship moved past the ships still at anchor, their crews crowded the decks and "sent up cheer after cheer." The Marines returned the cheers, but several of the older officers had their regrets. Major Henry C. Cochrane observed, "some of us felt anything but jolly at leaving behind the beauties of spring to be replaced by the perils of the sea and the hardships of war." On April 29, the *Panther* arrived at Key West.[7]

By now the country was officially at war. On April 30, a Spanish squadron under Admiral Pascual Cervera departed from the Portuguese Verde Islands. This departure of the Spanish fleet caused the Army to postpone indefinitely a planned "reconnaissance in force." The departure of the Spanish squadron may also have caused the postponement of a Marine landing in Cuba. Major Cochrane observed that the Marines had expected to "land in Cuba last Saturday [April 30], but now we must lie here."[8]

The news of Admiral George Dewey's victory at Manila Bay in the Philippines on May 1 reinforced the demand for a similar initiative in the Caribbean. The vanguard of any expedition was to be the force encamped at Tampa, Florida, under Army General William Shafter. But, as Secretary Long informed now Admiral Sampson on May 3, "no large army movement can take place until after we know the whereabouts of the Spanish."[9] Admiral Cervera's squadron remained a wild card.

The Marine battalion remained on board ship. When Huntington reported to Sampson, the latter could pass on no orders but stated "he did not want the Marines to go away to the Army. [He] had use for them." On May 3, Sampson departed from Key West with a small task force in the hopes of intercepting Cervera's squadron, leaving the Marine battalion to "fend for itself."[10]

At Key West, the Marine battalion settled into a routine of daily drills, almost-daily disputes with the Navy commander of the *Panther,* and rumormongering. Every morning the Marine battalion went ashore for drills. Most of the officers had served for many years in the Marine Corps, but the enlisted men were largely raw recruits. One Marine officer described a battalion parade as "a little Army, a little Navy, and some Marine Corps." Even Huntington stated that the men "have little idea of obeying orders."[11]

On May 23, the *Panther* received orders to tow a monitor out to sea. Forced to disembark when the ship sortied, the Marine battalion established a campsite on the beach. It was in effect marooned at Key West. Huntington futilely protested his forced "grounding." Meanwhile, his officers speculated about the future. The ubiquitous Major Cochrane spoke for many when he observed that the Marines "are not hurrying very much to get to

Cuba—unless we can have the prestige of being first."[12] But the Marine battalion's days at Key West were numbered.

On May 18, 1898, having eluded both Sampson's North Atlantic Squadron and Commodore Winfield Scott Schley's Flying Squadron, Admiral Cervera's small fleet entered the harbor of Santiago de Cuba on the southern coast of Cuba. On May 29, Schley, off Santiago, finally reported the "enemy in port."[13]

Secretary Long telegraphed Sampson at Key West, asking if the admiral could blockade Santiago and also seize Guantánamo Bay, about 40 miles to the east of the port. According to Sampson, after "the establishment of the blockade [of Santiago], my first thought was to find a harbor which could serve as . . . a base for the operations of the fleet." Whether at the urging of the department or on his own initiative, the admiral ordered the reembarkation of the Marine battalion.[14]

The Marines' forced inactivity at Key West caused some discord and bad press. The *New York Herald* wrote that the "Marines would rather eat than fight." By June 6, however, the battalion was back on board the *Panther,* which set sail the next morning to join the fleet off Santiago.[15]

Although their spirits were revived, the Marines still had no idea of their mission. On the morning of June 10, when the *Panther* joined the fleet, Admiral Sampson informed Huntington that the Marine battalion was to seize Guantánamo. Commander Bowman A. McCalla, commanding officer of the *Marblehead,* would serve as the overall commander of the expedition. Earlier the *Marblehead* had bombarded Spanish positions and landed a small reconnaissance detachment at Guantánamo under its Marine officer, Captain M. C. Goodrell. He selected a campsite on a hill near an abandoned Spanish blockhouse. On June 10, Goodrell briefed Huntington. According to Huntington, "we went ashore like innocents and made a peaceful camp and slept well."[16]

Although Marine pickets heard strange noises during the night, there was no other sign of any Spanish troops. The next morning, the Marines continued unloading their heavy equipment. Huntington and his officers were not too happy with the selection of their base camp. Although overlooking the water, it was on a hilltop clearing surrounded by dense underbrush. Captain McCawley, the battalion quartermaster, called the site "faulty" from a "military point of view." About 1,100 yards to the front was a larger ridgeline that dominated the Marine-held hill.[17]

The next evening and night, the Marines came under attack. About 1700, snipers killed two Marines on an outpost. Huntington sent out a patrol that found nothing. Still, the Marine commander felt secure. As he later wrote, "I do not know why I did not expect a night attack for we had a flurry in the P.M., but I did not." The enemy, however, returned. Major Cochrane, who had been directing the unloading operation on the beach, arrived with reinforcements. Before midnight the Spaniards only probed the outposts, but then initiated what Cochrane called "the beginning of 100 hours of fighting."[18]

The Navy surgeon with the battalion received a mortal wound in the first major attack. About daybreak, the enemy struck again and killed a Marine sergeant and wounded three other men. The fighting continued sporadically on June 12, but the Marines took no further casualties. Cochrane wrote his wife: "We have been having no end of racket and excitement. . . . We are all worn out with the tension of fighting the scoundrels all night and all day."[19]

With the continuing attacks on the afternoon of June 12, several of the Marine officers thought that the Spanish might overrun their camp. The Marines entrenched the top of the hill and moved their base camp to a lower site. Believing that the enemy was bringing up reinforcements, some of the company commanders even proposed that the battalion reembark. Major Cochrane argued forcibly against any such move, but Lieutenant Colonel Huntington remained noncommittal. Huntington referred the possibility of a withdrawal to Commander McCalla. Reputedly, the Navy officer replied, "you were put there to hold that hill. . . . If you're killed I'll come and get your dead body." The arrival of 60 friendly Cuban insurrectionists familiar with the terrain soon made the matter moot.[20]

Through June 13, the Spaniards harassed the Marine positions. According to the battalion's journal, "during the night persistent and trifling attacks were made on the camp in reply to which we used a good deal of ammunition." More bluntly, Major Cochrane wrote that there "was a vast deal of panicky, uncontrolled, and unnecessary fire." Again casualties were low, but the Marines lost their sergeant major, Henry Good, to a sniper.[21]

Lieutenant Colonel Huntington decided to take the offensive. The Cubans informed him that the enemy numbered between 400 and 500 troops. Their headquarters was six miles to the south, in the village of Cuzco, whose well was the Spaniards' only source of water. On June 14, Huntington sent two companies to destroy the well. Although moving through rugged terrain and encountering opposition, the Marines accomplished their mission supported by naval gunfire. In the fighting they sustained three wounded and several heat casualties. Their Cuban allies lost one man and suffered several wounded. The Marines captured a Spanish lieutenant and 17 enlisted men. According to the prisoners, the Spaniards had sustained heavy casualties. A few days later, Huntington sent out a 50-man patrol. He noted that "the expedition found many [enemy] dead but the intolerable stench from the dead made it impossible to continue search."[22]

With destruction of their water supply, the Spanish troops withdrew. The nearest enemy force, composed of 3,000 to 7,000 men, occupied the city of

Guantánamo 12 miles to the north. With Cuban insurrectionists in control of the countryside, the Americans had little to fear from the garrison. The Marines made an unspoken modus vivendi. As Huntington observed, "the Spaniards do not trouble us and [we] only talk of troubling them."[23]

Following the action of June 14, the Marine battalion spent the rest of its time at Guantánamo improving the camp. They also began to bask in the first publicity of their exploits. On the second day, several news correspondents arrived, including Stephen Crane, the novelist. American newspapers featured headlines reading, "First in the Fight" and "The Gallant Marines." Not lost on the public was the fact that the Marines had fought the Spanish while the Army forces under General Shafter still remained at Tampa.[24]

The question about the launching of the Army expedition against Cuba had preoccupied the military planners for some time. By the end of May, Shafter's V Corps was ready to deploy to Santiago. On May 31, the orders finally came. The troops were to embark in Army ships, which would then transport them to a position off Santiago, and then land either east or west of the city. Shafter was to move on Santiago, capture the Spanish garrison, and assist the Navy in the reduction of Cervera's squadron. Because of continuing difficulties with the embarkation, it was not until June 14 that the Army convoy set sail from Tampa.[25]

The first meeting between General Shafter and Admiral Sampson, on June 20, resulted in a misunderstanding. Both agreed to a landing at Daiquiri, only 18 miles southeast of Santiago, but according to Sampson, Shafter also "declared it to be his intention to attack the shore batteries [protecting the entrance to Santiago Bay] in the rear." Shafter denied this version and stated that the only feasible strategy had been to take the city first.[26]

The issue in dispute between the two commanders revolved around the Spanish fortifications. At the entrance to the bay, high cliffs dominated a narrow, winding channel. A Spanish minefield that restricted the water entryway, and gun batteries positioned on the eastern and western banks, known as the Morro and Socapa heights, respectively, supplemented these natural advantages. Admiral Sampson wanted the Army to attack the Morro heights while he used the Marine battalion and Marines from the fleet to take the Socapa heights. Such an attempt would have required close Army-Navy planning; it was not forthcoming.[27]

In the meantime, on June 22, Shafter's force came ashore. Opting for a decisive land battle, Shafter advanced upon the city of Santiago. On July 1, despite a tenuous line of communications, the American expeditionary corps defeated the Spanish in two hard-fought battles, San Juan Hill and El Caney. Shafter's victorious troops soon held the high ground overlooking Santiago. The Spanish force retreated into the city.[28]

Admiral Sampson and General Shafter, each concerned about the dangers to their respective forces, still remained far apart on objectives and strategy. On July 3, Sampson, on board the cruiser *New York,* headed for a meeting with Shafter. According to Captain French E. Chadwick, Sampson's chief of staff, the admiral was going to "explain the situation and lay out our plans . . . [to] carry the Morro by assault with a thousand Marines."[29]

The meeting with Shafter never took place. That day Admiral Cervera led his squadron out of Santiago in an attempt to reach the open sea. In the four-hour Battle of Santiago Bay, Sampson's force, temporarily under Commodore Schley, destroyed all of the Spanish ships.[30] The dispute between Shafter and Sampson remained unresolved. The Army had not yet taken the city of Santiago. At a conference with General Shafter on July 6, the Navy proposed that the Marine and Army troops capture the Socapa and Morro heights. Eventually an agreement of sorts was reached. The Navy would first shell the city of Santiago at long range. If the Spanish did not surrender, Marines from the fleet with the assistance of Cuban troops would attack the heights. At the same time, Sampson would attempt to force the entrance. It was unclear whether Shafter would provide troops.[31]

On July 10 and 11, Sampson's ships fired upon the city, but the admiral and the general soon reverted to their original positions. Shafter continued to want Sampson to close with the shore, but Sampson refused until the Army silenced the enemy artillery batteries.[32]

At the heart of the question was the feasibility of an assault on the Morro. Marine Major Robert L. Meade, who was the Fleet Marine Officer and who would have commanded the assault force on the Morro, for the most part agreed with Admiral Sampson. Examining the terrain after the surrender, he wrote: "The most difficult part . . . would be in reaching the crest from the beach. . . . An inferior force could conduct a defense with success . . . but as the army in the near vicinity had successfully assaulted positions similarly defended I was certain that my assault would have been successful also, if undertaken."[33]

Events, however, overtook the dispute. With continuing Army reinforcements from the United States, Shafter squeezed the vise. Finally, on July 15, after extended negotiations, the Spanish commander of Santiago agreed to surrender.

The 1st Marine Battalion remained at Guantánamo Bay. There, the Marines established a garrison routine. They manned their outposts, but encountered no enemy troops. The Marines maintained a high standard of health discipline, using only distilled water from the ships and burning their garbage. One of the first orders issued related to basic sanitary requirements: "Men are forbidden to ease themselves except at the latrine, and will not urinate inside the Fort." In contrast to the Army, the Marines did not suffer any cases of yellow fever and sustained only a 2 percent sickness rate.[34]

By the end of July, the Marine battalion was prepared to redeploy. The Navy wanted to extend the naval blockade to western Cuba and directed that the Marines seize the Isle of Pines as a "secure base." Lieutenant Colonel Huntington had some private doubts that some of the older officers would have the stamina for this additional operation.[35]

Fortunately for Huntington and his officers and men, they did not have to endure the hardships of further strenuous ground combat in a tropical climate. On August 9, the battalion departed Guantánamo on board Navy transport *Resolute,* escorted by the cruiser *Newark.* On August 12, the ships bombarded the city of Manzanillo west of Santiago, in a diversionary action. The news of the signing of the peace protocol calling for an armistice halted the proposed landing of the Marine battalion. The naval force stopped briefly at Guantánamo and then returned to the United States.[36]

Despite a somewhat rocky start at Guantánamo, the 1st Marine Battalion proved itself in combat. By seizing the heights at Guantánamo, it provided a safe anchorage for Navy ships. In effect, the Marines seized and protected an advance base for the fleet blockading Santiago.

The dispute between the Army and the Navy at Santiago provided important insight. It revealed that professional Army and Navy officers advocated different approaches. For General Shafter and his staff, the vital objective was capture of the Spanish garrison and the city of Santiago. On the other hand, the goal of Admiral Sampson and the Navy was the destruction of Cervera's fleet. General Shafter designed an overland campaign to capture the city and was unwilling to sacrifice men to take the Morro and Socapa heights. Similarly, Admiral Sampson refused to chance the loss of any of his ships by running the channel. Although both commanders attained their desired ends, their basic conflict remained unresolved. For the Navy, the message was clear that it required its own land force. It had this land force in the U.S. Marine Corps.

NOTES

1. SECNAV ltr to CMC and copy of ltr to C. A. Boutelle, Mar 10, 1898, Letters Received, "N," RG 127, National Archives and Records Administration (NARA); *Army and Navy Journal,* Mar 12, 1898, 515; Lieutenant Commander Richard Wainwright, "Our Naval Power," United States Naval Institute *Proceedings* (Mar 1898): 39–87, 48.
2. Lieutenant Colonel R. W. Huntington ltr to CMC, Feb 15, 1898, Letters Received, "N," RG 127, NARA.
3. Huntington ltr to Bobby, Mar 30, 1898, Colonel R. W. Huntington Papers, Marine Corps Historical Center (MCHC).

4. Long ltr to CinC, U.S. Naval Force, NA, Apr 6, 1898 and Sampson ltr to SECNAV, Apr 9, 1898 reprinted in *Appendix to the Report of the Chief of the Bureau of Navigation*, 171–73; David F. Trask, *The War with Spain in 1898* (London: Macmillan, 1981), 90–91; John D. Long, *The New American Navy* (New York: The Outlook Company, 1903), I, 243; Sampson at the time proposed a direct attack on Havana, but the idea was vetoed by Secretary Long. Captain Robley D. Evans, one of Sampson's officers, later wrote that he believed the fleet could have captured Havana two days after the declaration of war if Sampson's original plan had been followed. Captain A. T. Mahan, who joined the Navy's War Strategy Board after Assistant Secretary of the Navy Theodore Roosevelt resigned to form a volunteer regiment, defended the decision to implement the blockade: "Its importance lay in its two-fold tendency to exhaust the enemy's army in Cuba, and to force his navy to come to the relief. No effect more decisive than these two could be produced by us before the coming of the hostile navy, or the readiness of our own army to take the field." Robley D. Evans, *A Sailor's Log, Recollections of Forty Years of Naval Life* (New York: D. Appleton Company, 1910), 407; and A. T. Mahan, "The Naval War on the Sea and its Lessons," III, *McClures,* Dec 1898, 353–62, 357, in Printed Material Folder, H. C. Taylor Papers, LC. CMC ltrs to SECNAV, Apr 18 and 23, 1898, LSSN, v. 7, 250–52, and 266, RG 127, NARA; Acting CMC ltr to SECNAV, Apr 19, 1898, Letters Received, "N," RG 127, NARA; Entries for Apr 17–22, 1898 and Battalion Orders 1–3, Apr 19–20, 1898 in Journal of the Marine Battalion under Lieutenant Colonel Robert W. Huntington, Apr-Sep 1898, RG 127, NARA; CMC, *Annual Report, 1898,* 7 and 10; "Report of the Adjutant and Inspector of the USMC," Sep 20, 1898, in CMC *Annual Report, 1898,* 50 and 56; Charles L. McCawley, "The Marines at Guantánamo," n.d., MS, 2–4, Major General Charles L. McCawley Papers, MCHC; "Marine Battalion at Guantánamo," reprinted in *Appendix to the Report of the Chief of the Bureau of Navigation,* 440–41. Graham A. Cosmas observed that the "Marine mobilization coincides in time with the order for concentration of most of the Regular Army at Chickamauga Park, New Orleans, Mobile, and Tampa, which went out on 15 April." Graham A. Cosmas, comments on author's draft chapter, Mar 1990.

5. "Marines to Start Tonight," clipping from *Brooklyn Eagle,* Apr 22, 1898, General Clipping File, Cochrane Papers, MCHC; *New York Times,* Apr 23, 1898, 4; Charles L. McCawley, "The Marines at Guantánamo," n.d., MS 2–4, Major General Charles L. McCawley Papers, MCHC; "Marine Battalion at Guantánamo," reprinted in *Appendix to the Report of the Chief of the Bureau of Navigation,* 440–41; CMC, *Annual Report, 1898,* 6; CMC ltr to SECNAV, Apr 23, 1898, LSSN, v. 7, 250–52, RG 127, NARA; Cochrane ltr to Betsy, Apr 22, 1898, H. C. Cochrane Papers, MCHC.

6. Major George C. Reid ltr to Pendleton, Apr 19, 1898 in Major General Joseph H. Pendleton Papers, MCHC; Long msg to Sampson, Apr 21, 1898 reprinted in *Appendix to the Report of the Chief of the Bureau of Navigation,*

174–75; Cochrane ltr to Betsy, Apr 23, 1898, H. C. Cochrane Papers, MCHC; Long, *The New American Navy,* II, 5; Long promoted Sampson to the rank of rear admiral on April 21, 1898.

7. Entries for Apr 23–29, 1898 in *Journal of the Marine Battalion,* Apr-Sep 1898, RG 127, NARA; entries for Apr 23–18, 1898, Diary, H. C. Cochrane Papers, MCHC; Lieutenant Colonel R. W. Huntington rpt to CMC, Apr 30, 1898, Letters Received, Hist Sec, RG 127, NARA; McCawley, "The Marines at Guantánamo," 8–10; CMC, *Annual Report, 1898,* 6; Henry C. Cochrane ltr to Betsy, Apr 26, 1898, Folder 51, H. C. Cochrane Papers, MCHC.

8. While Spain officially declared war on the United States first, war was almost a certainty after April 11. That day President McKinley asked for the authority to employ U.S. military force if necessary. Congress on April 19 not only granted this authority but also recognized the independence of Cuba and demanded the withdrawal of the Spanish military forces from the island. Trask, *The War with Spain,* 53, 56, 162–63; Cosmas, *An Army for Empire,* 111–12; Leech, *In the Days of McKinley,* 198–99; Cochrane ltr to Betsy and boys, May 4, 1898, Cochrane Papers, MCHC; Huntington ltr to Bobby, Apr 30, 1898, R. W. Huntington Papers, MCHC.

9. Cosmas, *An Army for Empire,* 121–30; Leech, *In the Days of McKinley,* 214–16; Trask, *The War with Spain,* 163–67; Long ltr to Sampson, May 3, 1898 reprinted in *Appendix to the Report of the Chief of the Bureau of Navigation,* 366. Graham A. Cosmas observed that it was his understanding that "McKinley had unofficial reports of Dewey's victory at the time he began to revise strategy on May 2." Cosmas comments to author, Mar 1990.

10. Entry for Apr 30, 1898 in *Journal of the Marine Battalion,* Apr-Sep 1898, RG 127; McCawley, "The Marines at Guantánamo," 10; entry for May 3, 1898, Diary, H. C. Cochrane Papers, MCHC; Trask, *The War with Spain,* 114.

11. Entries for May 1–24, 1898 in *Journal of the Marine Battalion,* Apr-Sep 1898, RG 127, NARA; entry for May 31, 1898, Diary, H. C. Cochrane papers, MCHC; Huntington ltr to Bobby, May 27, 1898, R. W. Huntington Papers, MCHC.

12. Huntington ltrs to CMC, May 25 and Nov 3, 1898, Major Charles L. McCawley ltr to CMC, Jan 8, 1990, and Commodore George C. Remey endorsement to CMC, May 25, 1898, Letters Received, Historical, RG 127, NARA; Huntington ltr to Bobby, May 27, 1898, R. W. Huntington Papers, MCHC; Cochrane ltr to Betsy, May 6, 9, 12, 28, and Jun 1, 1898 and Betsy ltrs to Cochrane, Apr 24 and 25, 1898, Folder 51, Cochrane Papers, MCHC.

13. Exchange of messages between Long and Schley, May 27–29, 1898 reprinted in *Appendix to the Report of the Chief of the Bureau of Navigation,* 397–400.

14. Exchange of messages, May 28–30, 1898 reprinted in Ibid., 398–400; Rear Admiral William T. Sampson, "The Atlantic Fleet in the Spanish War," *Cen-*

tury Magazine, n. d., 886–913, 903 in Printed Material Folder, H. C. Taylor Papers, Library of Congress (LC).

15. Entries for Jun 1–7, 1898 in *Journal of the Marine Battalion,* Apr-Sep 1898, RG 127, NARA; entries for Jun 1–7, 1898, Cochrane Diary, H. C. Cochrane Papers, MCHC.

16. Entry for Jun 1–7, 1898, Cochrane Diary, H. C. Cochrane Papers, MCHC; McCalla ltr to Sampson, Jul 19, 1898 reprinted in Major Richard S. Collum, *History of the United States Marine Corps* (New York: R. L. Hamersly Co., 1903), 348–49; McCawley, "The Marines at Guantánamo," 9; Bernard C. Nalty, *The United States Marines in the War with Spain* (Washington: GPO, 1967 revised edition), 9; Huntington ltr to Bobby, Jun 19, 1898, R. W. Huntington Papers, MCHC.

17. McCawley, "The Marines at Guantánamo," 15–17.

18. Ibid.; entries for Jun 11–12, 1898, in *Journal of the Marine Battalion,* Apr-Sep 1898, RG 127, NARA; Huntington ltr to Bobby, Jun 19, 1898, R. W. Huntington Papers, MCHC; entries for Jun 11–12, 1898, Cochrane Diary, H. C. Cochrane Papers, MCHC.

19. Ibid.; Cochrane ltr to Wife, Jun 12, 1898, Folder 51, H. C. Cochrane Papers, MCHC.

20. Entries for Jun 11–12, 1898, in *Journal of the Marine Battalion,* Apr-Sep 1898, RG 127, NARA. The discussion about the proposed evacuation is contained in Cochrane's diary (entries for Jun 11–12, 1898, and in flysheet in back of diary for 1898, H. C. Cochrane Papers, MCHC), which refers to interviews with several other witnesses. He also mentions the incident in a letter to his wife (Cochrane ltr to Wife, Jun 14, 1898, Folder 51, Cochrane Papers, MCHC). Cochrane was not a witness to McCalla's refusal and gives conflicting accounts. In a separate report, Commander McCalla only stated: "The mistake of locating the camp between the main position and the outpost was corrected . . . at my suggestion." McCalla ltr to Sampson, Jul 19, 1898 reprinted in Collum, *History of the United States Marine Corps,* 348–49.

21. Entries for Jun 12–13, 1898 in *Journal of the Marine Battalion,* Apr-Sep 1898, RG 127, NARA; entry for Jun 13, 1898, Cochrane Diary, Cochrane Papers, MCHC.

22. Entries for Jun 14, 19, 1898, in *Journal of the Marine Battalion,* Apr-Sep 1898, RG 127, NARA.

23. McCawley, "The Marines at Guantánamo," 31–37; McCalla ltr to CinC North Atlantic Station, Jun 16, 1898, Letters Received, Hist Section, RG 127, NARA; Sampson ltr to Long, Jun 22, 1898, reprinted in *Appendix to the Report of the Chief of the Bureau of Navigation,* 449; Huntington ltr to Bobby, Jul 4, 1898, R. W. Huntington Papers, MCHC.

24. *Journal of the Marine Battalion,* Apr-Sep 1898, RG 127, NARA; McCawley, "The Marines at Guantánamo," 28, 31–40, 1898; entries for Jun 13–15, 1898, Cochrane Diary, H. C. Cochrane Papers, MCHC; Clippings, "First to Fight" and "The Gallant Marines," n.d., n.p., General Clipping File,

H. C. Cochrane Papers, MCHC; R. W. Stallman and E. R. Hageman, eds., *The War Despatches of Stephen Crane* (New York: Macmillan, 1964), 140–54, 171–72, 267–74; Captain G. F. Elliott ltr to Huntington, Jun 18, 1898, reprinted in CMC, *Annual Report, 1898,* 29; William E. Nanscawen, Spanish American War Survey, n. d., U.S. Military Collection, U.S. Army Military History Institute Collection, Carlisle Barracks, PA; Allan R. Millett, *Semper Fidelis: The History of the United States Marine Corps* (New York: Free Press, 1981), 133–34.

25. Long msg to Sampson, May 31, 1898 quoted in Sampson, Report of Operations of the North Atlantic Fleet, Aug 3, 1898 reprinted in *Appendix to the Report of the Chief of the Bureau of Navigation,* 480; Trask, *The War with Spain,* 175–76, 182–88; Cosmas, *An Army for Empire,* 181, 195–97.

26. Sampson is quoted from Sampson, "The Atlantic Fleet in the Spanish War," 904–5. See also Sampson ltr to Long, Jun 22, 1898 reprinted in *Appendix to the Report of the Chief of the Bureau of Navigation,* 450–51. Although Sampson refers to the meeting of June 20 in the latter source, he does not state the objective of the Army task force once it lands. Shafter is quoted in Trask, *The War with Spain,* 204. See also Cosmas, *An Army for Empire,* 205–6.

27. Trask, *The War with Spain,* 199–205. See also Cosmas, *An Army for Empire,* 177, 205–9.

28. Cosmas, *An Army for Empire,* 209–16. See also Trask, *The War with Spain,* 225–52.

29. Chadwick ltr to Cornelia Chadwick, Jul 4, 1898 in Doris D. Maguire, ed., *French Ensor Chadwick, Selected Letters and Papers* (Washington: University Press of America, 1981), 194–95.

30. Trask, *The War with Spain,* 261–69.

31. "Minutes of a conversation between Captain Chadwick of the Navy, representing Admiral Sampson, and General Shafter," Jul 6, 1898, reproduced in Sampson, Report of Operations, Jul 15, 1898, 610. Chadwick, in his history, however, states that Shafter had agreed to attack the Morro. French Ensor Chadwick, *The Relations of the United States with Spain, The Spanish American War,* 2 vols. (New York: Russell & Russell, 1911, reissued in 1968), 208. David Trask agrees with Chadwick that Shafter agreed to attack the Morro, "although for unexplained reasons this aspect of the plan was not made explicit in the minutes of the meeting." Trask, *The War with Spain,* 293. Graham Cosmas comments that from "3 July on, Shafter was engaged in his own negotiations with the Spanish commander, General Toral, looking to the surrender of the garrison. I'm not sure how thoroughly, or even whether, he kept Sampson filled in on this." Cosmas comments to author, Mar 1990.

32. Long, *New Navy,* II, 152; Long ltr to Sampson, Jul 13, 1898 in Rear Admiral W. T. Sampson, "History of Relations between Army and Navy at Santiago," Aug 1, 1898 reprinted in *Appendix to the Report of the Chief of the Bureau of Navigation,* 625; Trask, *The War with Spain,* 301, 306–8.

33. Lieutenant Colonel Robert L. Meade ltr to Major Charles L. McCawley, Mar 18, 1899, Charles L. McCawley Papers, MCHC.

34. 1st Marine Bn Order No. 3, Jun 21, 1898, *Journal of the Marine Battalion,* Apr–Sep 1898, RG 127, NARA; McCawley, "The Marines at Guantánamo," 45–48; Cochrane ltr to Betsy, Jul 23, 1898, Cochrane Papers, MCHC.

35. A. T. Mahan, "The War on the Sea and Its Lessons," *McClures,* n.d., 527–34, 532 in Printed Material Folder, H. C. Taylor Papers, Library of Congress; Huntington ltr to Bobby, Jul 29, 1898, R. W. Huntington Papers, MCHC.

36. F. Goodrich ltr to CinC North Atlantic Fleet, Aug 13, 1898, reprinted in *Appendix to the Report of the Chief of the Bureau of Navigation,* 301–3.

NINE

"THE MEN BEHIND THE GUNS"

THE IMPACT OF THE WAR WITH SPAIN ON THE NAVY ENLISTED FORCE

JAMES R. RECKNER

"A chain is never any stronger than its weakest link, and the men behind the guns are a very important link in the chain of defense which our Navy has linked around us."[1]

IMMENSE PRESTIGE ACCRUED TO THE U.S. NAVY and thus the men of the fleet as a result of the battles of Manila Bay and Santiago de Cuba. "One of Dewey's Men" was a description the sailors of the Asiatic Squadron who were present at the Battle of Manila Bay proudly attached to themselves evermore.[2] The Navy and the men who served in it were beneficiaries of much good will as a result of the Navy's apparent readiness for war. This appearance of readiness was emphasized by the Army's equally apparent lack of readiness. And, of course, the fleet victories seemed to confirm these perceptions, although later critical analysis of American gunnery at the principal battles suggested the hitting rate of the American guns was less than stellar. Objective criticism, however, was unwelcome, and even a decade after the war, when Commander William S. Sims cited the gunnery figures during Senate hearings, he was roundly condemned.

At other levels, the impact of the war on the enlisted force was mixed. During this decade of institutional indifference toward the needs of the enlisted man, the enlisted force grew very rapidly, from an authorized strength of 13,500 in 1898 to 44,000 in 1909. The dynamic for this growth was a direct development of the war: the rapid growth of the fleet to meet the new defense requirements of empire. While a remarkable amount of public discussion and interest was focused upon the development of the battleship fleet during the decade following the war with Spain, much less attention was paid to the problem of who would man these new ships. And these were ships that had a seemingly unquenchable thirst for men and yet more men to perform a wide range of increasingly technological skills, the likes of which the sailors of the "Old Navy" could only marvel.

As the fleet grew, Congress almost annually—and always grudgingly—increased the Navy's authorized personnel strength, but never by the amount the Navy Department felt sufficient to fully man the ships under construction. I suspect this congressional reluctance hardly mattered; throughout the period the Bureau of Navigation was unable to meet the Navy's authorized strength, even as bureau officials complained it was too low.[3]

In 1901, realizing they could no longer meet their personnel needs by recruiting from the traditional methods in the seaports of the world, the Navy began sending recruiting parties to cities in the interior of the United States. These recruits represented a new class within the Navy. The great majority of them had at least a public school education. They came, Commander William G. Miller advised Secretary of the Navy Truman H. Newberry in 1909, "from the same class of people from which officers are taken and [their] average intelligence is equal to the average intelligence, less the superior education, of the officers in the navy."[4] These new men, Rear Admiral Charles S. Sperry wrote in 1909, were enlisted "from the very pick and choice of the whole country." Pay, in itself, was not sufficient enticement. "The men we must have enlist largely from a spirit of adventure, a desire to see the world, stimulated by a very considerable amount of patriotic pride."[5]

Unfortunately, there were no scientific studies of recruits' motivation to join the Navy, but the heroic image projected by the Navy's victories in the war with Spain must have been a powerful contributing factor. New York's tumultuous reception of Rear Admiral William T. Sampson's North Atlantic Squadron on its return from Cuba in 1898 and the popular craze associated with Admiral George Dewey's triumphal return from the Philippines in 1899 undoubtedly strengthened the Navy's appeal.

These events attracted a generation of young men of recruiting age during the era of Theodore Roosevelt, many of whom longed for the broadening experience of overseas travel and adventure. The publication of extensive reports on the progress of building the new battleship fleet; the Navy's role in lifting the Boxer siege of the legations in Peking; and colorful and exciting accounts of cruises such as the North Atlantic Squadron's voyage to European waters in 1903, must have confirmed the popular image of the Navy. And, of course, the world cruise of the Atlantic Fleet (the Great White Fleet) from December 1907 to February 1909 was the most compelling illustration of navy life as an exciting adventure—it was a recruiting officer's dream come true.

Additionally, naval fiction flourished as a popular genre, with a number of works published by naval officers such as Yates Sterling Jr. and Edward L. Beach (father of the current Captain Edward L. Beach, USN [Ret.]). These highly popular accounts further publicized the Navy amongst the critical target audience—America's youth. Firsthand accounts of enlisted life in the Navy,[6] a crop of autobiographical works by prominent officers,[7] and books relating to the world cruise of the Great White Fleet[8] sustained interest in the Navy as a career.

The Navy acted aggressively to convert young men's passive desire for travel and adventure into an active commitment to serve in the Navy. In addition to permanent recruiting stations and traveling recruiting parties, the Navy circulated 150,000 large lithographic billboard posters advertising the advantages of joining the Navy. Additionally, naval leaders sought to have good stories about the Navy published in newspapers, and recruiting officers developed very innovative strategies to locate potential recruits.[9]

By various methods, recruiters managed to attract a large number of candidates to the recruiting office. There, a surprising percentage were rejected for physical and other reasons, such as illiteracy, with the result that throughout the period an average of nearly 74 percent of applicants were rejected or otherwise failed to enlist.[10] Despite the remarkably high rejection rate, men either physically unfit or illiterate still managed to enter the service. A surgeon who joined the receiving ship *Independence* at Mare Island, California, in 1903, complained to the Surgeon General that *Independence* was "being overwhelmed by a tide of recruits physically unsuited for service." Of the recruits on board upon his arrival, the surgeon discharged 8 outright for medical reasons and sent an additional 14 to the Mare Island Naval Hospital for treatment or survey.[11] In yet another case, an officer of the Atlantic Training Squadron reported that one of his ships had received 9 recruits from the receiving ship *Franklin* who were unable to read or write. The squadron's chaplain was assigned the duty to teach them, but as the commander reported, "gross carelessness on the part of the enlisting officers must be apparent."[12]

These developments are reflections of the pressure under which recruiting officers labored as they struggled to meet the Navy's ever-growing needs. They suggest, too, that little time was devoted to ensuring the applicants met the Navy's many requirements; that they were neither deserters nor felons, had never been dishonorably discharged, could read and write, and were of good character. Under pressure to produce numbers, it can be speculated that the surgeons who traveled with the recruiting officers also were encouraged to "overlook" some medical conditions that were otherwise disqualifying.[13]

ENLISTMENT OF MINORITIES

In the midst of this pressure to recruit men, one might suspect that the Navy would turn with interest toward racial minorities. In fact, this did not happen. To be sure, there were racial minorities in Theodore Roosevelt's Navy, and the President once hosted a luncheon at the White House for the crews (including black crew members) of two of the ships that served him directly. The Bureau of Navigation annually reported the racial composition of the enlisted force, and although they did not keep a record of the number of black petty officers, according to a 1910 report it was "known that there [were] several."[14] These annual figures indicate that the actual number of blacks in the service remained fairly constant throughout the period, but due to the rapid increase in overall enlisted strength, blacks declined as a percentage of the total enlisted force from 5.8 percent in 1904 to 3.4 percent in 1909.[15]

No detailed information is available concerning the specific distribution of these blacks within the various enlisted ratings; however, a 1913 report provides an insight. In response to a request from an African American pastor to know whether black sailors would be marching in the Wilson inaugural parade, Rear Admiral Philip Andrews, responding in the negative, explained that the ships sending contingents to the inaugural had in their complements a total of 152 blacks. Of these, 21 were in the engine room force, 6 in the commissary branch, 122 were in the mess attendant branch, and 3 were gunners' mates.[16] These figures provide an interesting indication of the relative proportion of blacks in various specialties in the Navy, although the figures are far from definitive:

Clearly, the black sailors' principal role in the early twentieth century Navy was in the mess attendant branch. This branch, which encompassed all officers' cooks and stewards, was subjected to continuing scrutiny by the officers, for these were the men who performed all of the officers' personal tasks.

Even before the war with Spain propelled the Navy into a large role in Asian waters, Chinese and Japanese men were preferred as mess attendants. After the war, significant changes occurred. The Navy Department intro-

Table 9.1　Distribution of Blacks by Specialty, Battleships *New Hampshire* and
　　　　　　Louisiana, 1913

Mess	122	80.3%
Engine room	21	13.8%
Commissary	6	3.9%
Gunnery	3	2.0%

duced a program to eliminate aliens from the service, first prohibiting reenlistment of men who had not formally declared their intention to seek citizenship,[17] and then, in 1908, forbidding altogether the enlistment or reenlistment of aliens.[18] These policies had the effect of greatly reducing the number of European and South American citizens in the U.S. Navy. However, in the mess attendant rating, too few white and/or native-born Chinese Americans and Japanese Americans applied, so initially Japanese and Chinese were exempted because of their "special value."[19]

Of the two Oriental groups, the Chinese were much favored, but the Chinese Exclusion Acts made their retention difficult. Nevertheless, commanding officers continued to enlist Chinese as mess attendants, with the result that a floating population of Chinese enlisted men existed on the Asiatic Station. These individuals were prohibited from entering the United States, even though they were fully enlisted members of our Navy.

The second preferred option for officers' stewards was Japanese, for whom the complications of the Exclusion Acts did not apply. However, American officers considered Japanese servants "inferior and much less desirable than Chinese."[20] Following the Japanese defeat of Russia and the emergence of Japan as America's principal Pacific rival, the continuing difficulties with employing Chinese and a growing concern that Japanese servants on board American ships presented a potential "fifth column"[21] threat inspired naval officers to seek other sources for mess attendants.

In June 1907, at the height of the war scare with Japan, Captain Vincendon J. Cottman reported, "there is a general complaint throughout the service regarding the unsuitability of [Japanese] mess attendants," and recommended recruiting one hundred or more young Filipinos "suitable for instruction" and training them at a school to be established on board the receiving ship *Independence* at Mare Island. This course of action, Cottman suggested, would solve this "much vexed and annoying problem."[22]

Initially, no action was taken on this recommendation. However, by the summer of 1907, with the impending departure of the Atlantic battleship fleet for the Pacific, the issue of Japanese stewards again occupied the minds of many officers. Although not all Japanese were transferred from the fleet, in the last days before the Atlantic Fleet departed for its world cruise, all Japanese cooks, stewards, and mess attendants in excess of allowance, who had been transferred to the battleships for further transfer to the ships of the Pacific Fleet, were transferred to the receiving ship *Franklin* in Norfolk.[23] On December 11, 1907, the Bureau of Navigation authorized recruitment of Filipinos and Puerto Ricans for service as mess attendants.[24]

Unfortunately, this policy change came too late to be of assistance to the departing fleet. A number of blacks therefore were hastily recruited to serve in the fleet's ward rooms. Inadequately trained, the new black mess attendants served only to confirm officers' preexisting prejudices. Under such circumstances began the long association of Filipinos and Chamorros (natives of Guam) with the ward rooms of the U.S. Navy. Enlistment of Filipinos increased rapidly, with 901 in service in 1909. Filipinos first outnumbered blacks in 1914, and continued to do so until the late 1930s, at times numbering more than nine times the black strength.

LEADERSHIP AND A SAILOR'S LIFE IN TR'S NAVY

The growth in size and increase in necessary education levels of the enlisted force during this period should have engaged the full attention of the Navy Department leadership. Unfortunately, this was not the case. As Frederick Harrod has so clearly pointed out, throughout the period from before the Spanish-American War to World War II, there was only one Secretary of the Navy who expressed a sustained interest in the welfare of the enlisted men; that was Josephus Daniels, Woodrow Wilson's Secretary of the Navy (1913–1921).[25] The secretaries who filled the position in the immediate post-Spanish-American War years—and they were many, with six during the Theodore Roosevelt presidency alone—expressed a patronizing sort of interest, particularly in correspondence with disgruntled parents of enlisted men experiencing difficulties in their service. However, they initiated no significant programs to aid them.

Lacking secretarial interest, the fate of the enlisted men fell to the chief of the Navy bureau responsible for them, the Bureau of Navigation. It might reasonably have been expected that here one would find an official dedicated to improving sailors' lives and ameliorating the conditions, often harsh, under which they worked. In reality, none of the chiefs of the Bureau of Navigation during the decade following the war with Spain expressed any particular understanding of the enlisted men's problems. They remained content with long-held attitudes, forged during decades of service after the Civil War, that the quality of the enlisted men had improved significantly. They were blissfully unaware that such change necessitated a change in officer leadership. Yet that very lack of understanding, it now seems apparent, contributed to the seriousness of the problems of the enlisted force, for throughout the decade after 1898, desertion remained at a nearly constant 14 to 15 percent per annum, thus exacerbating the already difficult task of manning the fleet.

"In them days," former Navy Seaman Arch Adamson recalled, "you so much as winked and you got clapped in double irons."[26] While it is tempting to discount Adamson's account as the typical complaints of an enlisted man, statistics actually bear him out. For the year ending June 30, 1905, the cruiser *Minneapolis,* with a crew of 477, reenlisted only 4 men, while she discharged 60 and had 56 deserters, for a net loss of 116 men, or 23 percent of her crew. She also had 1 general court martial and 68 summary courts. Under the category "petty" punishments, her commanding officer reported that 114 men spent a total of 668 nights in double irons, another 60 spent 250 days in solitary confinement on bread and water, and 188 men received extra duty. It is notable that confinement in double irons was considered "petty punishment"! The total number of desertions, courts martial, and "petty" punishments in a single year (487) exceeded by ten the number of men in her crew![27] Yet these figures were unremarkable. The battleship *Massachusetts,* with a crew of 561, during the same period reported 11 enlistments, 55 discharges, 99 desertions, 9 general and 159 summary courts martial, and a staggering 2,559 "petty" punishments, for a total deserters/punishments figure of 2,812, or an average of 5 punishments for each and every member of the crew! And these figures were for but a single year![28]

When one of the commanding officers of the receiving ships, which were the period's equivalent of recruit training centers and brigs, was bold enough to suggest that he conduct systematic interviews of newly returned deserters to see what had motivated them to leave the service, his suggestion was rejected by the Chief of the Bureau of Navigation, Rear Admiral Henry Clay Taylor. Taylor was then much heralded as the leading intellectual of the Navy of the period, the man who actually implemented the concept of concentration of the battleship fleet in the Atlantic during his tenure as Chief of the Bureau of Navigation. But Taylor felt systematic study of the complex issue of desertion was unnecessary. He was convinced that the "largest element" of the problem was "the restlessness of the average American young man, and the easy way in which he can get employment and, therefore, the readiness with which he drops any position he may hold."[29] The fault, as Taylor and most officers saw it, reported the rebuffed officer, "was held to exist in human nature, which is immutable, and not in naval conditions, which may be changed—unquestionably a most comforting deduction."[30]

Indeed, a reading of the surviving records and correspondence of the officer corps of the U.S. Navy during the decade following the war with Spain provides stunning evidence, through its general lack of reference to the enlisted men, that they simply were not a significant concern of the officers who led them. While the officers were wont to boast of the high quality of American enlisted men, they failed to recognize that the leadership approaches that had worked during the age of sail when the Navy had wooden ships and iron men were inappropriate for an enlisted force increasingly better educated and more technology oriented.

Discussing desertion, Rear Admiral Charles D. Sigsbee (who had commanded the *Maine* at the time of her sinking in 1898) noted in 1903 that many recent recruits were not fully informed of the consequences of desertion—loss of the right to hold any public office, loss of rights as citizens, etc. "It seems cruel," Sigsbee told Secretary of the Navy William H. Moody, "to inflict punishments on young men not properly informed of their liabilities in the matter of desertion." Nevertheless, Sigsbee supported just that. "I beg to submit that leniency in respect to desertion is likely to work harm to the service. *Inflexible precedent has much to do with the support of those in authority*" (emphasis added).[31] The same "inflexible precedent" guided Captain Charles M. Thomas in his command of the receiving ship *Franklin*. There, every sailor absent without leave, regardless of reason, received a summary court martial. Every sailor, including those just reporting on board, was inspected; every nonregulation uniform item was confiscated and immediately destroyed. As most uniforms were handmade at this time, the nonregulation aspects might easily have been corrected without significant expense; thus, this treatment hardly created an environment conducive to contented enlisted men.

As one enlisted man on board Captain Thomas's ship complained, "it's hard to be cussed, cheated out of our wage, [and] confined to the brig if we cry out against such treatment." Concerning officer attitudes toward enlisted men, F. E. Elkins continued, "we salute our officers but don't know what it is for one to return a salute. It seems as if they were leagued together to tyrannize over [*sic*] the poor fellows."[32] Echoing this sentiment, Captain Albert C. Dillingham in 1906 reported that desertion stemmed from the "lack of personal interest on the part of divisional officers in the welfare of the men of their division."[33] This was an essential relationship that was all too often missing, even though its importance was known. As one petty officer commented concerning one of the Navy's happy ships, the battleship *Louisiana,* "the officers made the crew, and the crew made a home of the ship."[34]

Far too many senior officers failed to recognize the sea change that had occurred in the enlisted force. "Inflexible precedent" might have been very comforting to the senior officers, but to a class of men able to read and write and evaluate the justice and rationality of events on board their ships, the application of logic to the system of discipline would have been much more effective as a method to maintain "the support of those in authority." The officer corps' failure to grasp this very basic principle constituted a leadership failure of staggering proportions, and contributed in a very large way to the flood of desertions throughout the period. This, in turn, added very significantly to the enlistment burden as the Navy struggled to man the rapidly growing fleet. So great did that burden become that in 1907 commissioning of the new battleship *Georgia* and the cruiser *St. Louis* was delayed until sufficient crewmembers could be found.[35] The Navy also found it necessary to decommission two older battleships simply to find sufficient crew members to send the rest of the fleet on the cruise around the world.[36]

Even when in extremis, the senior officer corps refused to acknowledge realities. Reporting on shortages in the Pacific Fleet in September 1907, Rear Admiral William T. Swinburne noted personnel shortages of as much as 132 men in a cruiser's crew of 300. Rather than examine causes of enlisted discontent, he reported "enlistments and reenlistments are very few on this station, owing to the unusual high wage paid for skilled and unskilled labor."[37] Once again personnel shortages were attributed to immutable factors, rather than Navy conditions.

In 1906 an enlisted man on board the battleship *Louisiana* wrote a stinging assessment of the officer corps:

> There are a few officers in this outfit who have the first principles of a square deal in their composition, but they are most woefully few and seldom. Their training at Annapolis seems to make the worst kind of snobs of them. They get the idea that the flatfoot is some kind of an animal to be driven and not led; and the sea service they get as midshipmen . . . helps them along the same lines.[38]

As "One of Dewey's Men" wrote from the Pacific Station in 1902, "we . . . would be the best drilled Navy in the world, as we were once, if the after part of the ship [officer's country] were hauled out for the sun of investigation to shine on it for a little while."[39]

In sum, the war with Spain and subsequent developments caused a period of sustained growth of the U.S. Navy and, concomitantly, its enlisted force. Achievement of the congressionally mandated enlisted levels remained beyond the Navy's ability throughout the first decade of the twentieth century for a number of complex and conflicting reasons. The war energized the drive to "Americanize"—and thus to narrow the pool of potential recruits—even while the Navy was enlarging. And though a pool of American citizens existed in the African American community, this potential source remained largely untapped throughout the period, a sad reflection of American attitudes of the day. Again, the war, and the advent of empire, offered the Navy an "easy out" by enlisting Filipinos, Puerto Ricans, and Chamorros instead of African Americans, thereby prolonging the day of reckoning in racial matters.

Remarkably, of those white Americans willing to enlist, a very large percentage proved physically or intellectually unfit for service. Compounding all of the above was the conservative—perhaps even reactionary—attitude of the American officer corps that, though decrying the problems of maintaining the enlisted force, remained curiously detached and disinterested in scientifically studying and resolving the problems that beset the force.

NOTES

1. "Praise for the Blue Jacket," *Army and Navy Register* 38 (Jul 1, 1905): 27.
2. See, for example, "One of Dewey's Men, 'The Blue Jacket's Point of View,'" *Army and Navy Journal* 34 (Mar 24, 1902): 756–57.
3.

Number of Petty Officers, Seamen, Landsmen, Boy, etc., Authorized and Actual

	Authorized	Actual		Authorized	Actual
1898	13,500	22,828	1904	34,000	29,321
1899	20,000	14,501	1905	37,000	30,804
1900	20,000	16,832	1906	37,000	32,163
1901	25,050	18,825	1907	38,500	33,027
1902	28,000	21,433	1908	44,500	39,048
1903	31,000	27,245	1909	44,500	42,861

Source: Pittman Pulsifier, Comp., *Navy Yearbook: Compilation of Annual Naval Appropriation Laws from 1883 to 1909* (Washington: GPO, 1909), 678–79. This information is presented in Frederick S. Harrod, *Manning the New Navy: The Development of a Modern Naval Enlisted Force, 1899–1940* (Westport, CT: Greenwood Press, 1978), 198. Harrod's work remains the most comprehensive study of the Navy's enlisted force.

4. Commander William G. Miller, CO, *Minnesota,* to Newberry, Feb 9, 1909, National Archives, Record Group 24, Entry 88, File 1159, Document 267 (hereafter NA, RG 24:88/1159–267).
5. Rear Admiral C. S. Sperry, manuscript, "Cruise of the U.S. Atlantic Fleet," 13, Sperry Papers, Naval Historical Foundation Collection, Library of Congress (hereafter NHF, LC). Sperry commanded the Great White Fleet during the second half of its cruise around the world, 1907–1909.
6. See, for example, L. G. T., *Three Years Behind the Guns: The True Chronicles of a "Diddy-Box"* (New York: The Century Co., 1908). Although not available to the youth of the era, a new work, *A Rocky Mountain Sailor in Teddy*

Roosevelt's Navy: The Letters of Petty Officer Charles Fowler from the Asiatic Station, 1905–1910, Rodney G. Tomlinson, ed. (Boulder, CO: Westview Press, 1998), gives a good account of contemporary enlisted life.

7. Perhaps the most popular officer of the day, Rear Admiral Robley D. "Fighting Bob" Evans, managed his autobiography in two volumes! Evans, *A Sailor's Log: Recollections of Forty Years of Naval Life* (New York: D. Appleton & Co., 1911).

8. Here, see particularly Franklin Matthews's two-volume account: *With the Battle Fleet: Cruise of the Sixteen Battleships of the United States Atlantic Fleet from Hampton Roads to the Golden Gate, December 1907–May 1908* (New York: B. W. Huebsch, 1908); and *Back to Hampton Roads: Cruise of the United States Atlantic Fleet from San Francisco to Hampton Roads, July 7, 1908–February 22, 1909* (New York: B. W. Huebsch, 1909).

9. See, for examples, *Army and Navy Register* 32 (Sep 20, 1902): 2, and 39 (Jun 16, 1906): 12. For recruiting strategy, see Lieutenant Commander D. W. Coffman to ChBuNav, Dec 16, 1904, NA, RG 24:88/525–198.

10.

Enlistments, 1899–1909

	Applied	Enlisted
1899	41,756	8,270 (19.8%)
1900	40,854	8,123 (19.9%)
1901	38,998	9,896 (25.4%)
1902	37,043	10,294 (27.8%)
1903	47,765	12,934 (27.1%)
1904	40,709	13,380 (32.9%)
1905	41,239	11,719 (28.4%)
1906	40,918	13,418 (32.9%)
1907	45,691	14,329 (31.4%)
1908	80,442	21,929 (26.9%)
1909	91,588	18,713 (20.4%)
Total	547,003	142,995 (26.1%)

Source: Harrod, *op. cit.,* 176, citing annual reports of the Chief of the Bureau of Navigation. Harrod contains a detailed breakdown of rejections, waivers, and failures to enlist.

11. Surgeon General P. Kindleberger to Surgeon General Presley M. Rixey, Sep 25, 1903, NA, RG 24:88/525–94.

12. Rear Admiral William C. Wise to ChBuNav (Rear Admiral George Converse) Oct 14, 1904, NA, RG 24:88/525–180.

13. See Harrod, *op. cit.,* 51, for detailed discussion.

14. BuNav to Lewis H. Blair, Richmond, VA, Nov 19, 1910, NA, RG 24:88/529–47. The bureau's ability to produce these numbers suggests some

specific record identifying individual blacks existed, but this record, if it did exist, has not been located.

15.

	Blacks	Total Force	Percentage
1904	1,700	29,321	5.8%
1906	1,456	30,804	4.7%
1907	1,484	32,163	4.6%
1908	1,867	39,048	4.8%
1909	1,768	42,861	4.1%
1910	1,535	45,076	3.4%

Source: Harrod, *op. cit.,* 181, citing ChBuNav annual reports. The 1904 figure is noted on R.R. Wright, Georgia State Industrial College to SecNav (Morton), Dec 21, 1904, NA, RG 24:88/523–69. Contradicting these figures, in 1903 the *Army & Navy Journal* reported that only 500 blacks were on duty in the Navy. 500/27,245 = 1.8%. *Army & Navy Journal* 40 (Aug 8, 1903): 1229.

16. Rear Admiral Andrews, Acting SecNav, to Rev. J. Milton Waldron, Feb 7, 1913, NA, RG 24:88/525–60.
17. *Army & Navy Register* 36 (Oct 29, 1904): 1.
18. SecNav Victor H. Metcalf memo to BuNav, Jan 4, 1908, NA, RG 24:88/5525–79.
19. *Army & Navy Register* 36 (Oct 29, 1904): 1.
20. Captain John Robinson endorsement, Nov 14, 1907, to Lieutenant William H. Standley to Robinson, NA, RG 24:88/5325–21.
21. For examples of this concern, see W. P. C. Adams to Theodore Roosevelt, Feb 20, 1906, NA, RG 24:88/5325–1; W. T. Parker to Roosevelt, Jun 16, 1907, NA, RG 24:88/5325–22. Many naval officers shared this fear.
22. Cottman, Captain of Puget Sound Yard, to SecNav, Jun 4, 1907, NA, RG 24:88/5325–6. Two hundred to three hundred Filipinos had already been employed as crew members of the Insular Naval Force; they complicate calculation of numbers recruited for mess attendant, but assuming the 285 Filipinos in service in 1906 constituted the Insular Force, then Filipinos for mess attendant were roughly as follows:

		Mess Attendant	
	Total	Filipinos	Chamorros
1906	285	0	28
1907	399	114	37
1908	455	165	38
1909	901	616	51
1910	969	684	76

Source: Harrod, *op. cit.,* 183.

23. Commander Henry B. Wilson (BuNav) to CinC Atlantic Fleet (Rear Admiral Evans), Dec 7, 1908, NA, RG 24:88/1754–457.

24. SecNav memorandum to BuNav, Jan 4, 1908, NA, RG 24:88/5525–79. The order was issued verbally on Dec 11, 1907, as noted on the written order of Jan 4.

25. Frederick C. Harrod, *Manning the New Navy,* 26–30.

26. Arch Adamson, "Impressions," Navy Department Library.

27. USS *Minneapolis* Annual Report, Jul 10, 1905, NA, RG 45:464, File O, Box 473.

28. CinC Atlantic Fleet [Rear Admiral Evans] Annual Report, Sep 12, 1905, NA, RG 45:464/OO, Box 473.

29. Taylor to SecNav William H. Moody, Jul 29, 1902, Moody Papers, vol. 2, NHF, LC. Rear Admiral J. B. Coughlin repeated this same justification, almost verbatim, in an article, "What the Navy Is and What It Needs," published in the Philadelphia *Public Ledger* and extracted in *Army & Navy Journal* 42 (Apr 1, 1905): 826.

30. Rear Admiral Caspar F. Goodrich, "Desertions in the Navy," *Army & Navy Register* 39 (Mar 17, 1906): 26–27.

31. Sigsbee to Moody, Aug 28, 1903, NA, RG 24:88/3711–3.

32. F. E. Elkins, USS *Franklin,* to Navy Department, Apr 4, 1903, NA, RG 24:88/3328–1.

33. Dillingham to ChBuNav (Rear Admiral George A. Converse), Aug 7, 1906, NA, RG 24:88/1159–101.

34. Electrician 1st Class John M. Buris, quoted in "Letters from the Enlisted Men of the Navy," *Army & Navy Register* 44 (Aug 29, 1908): 21.

35. *Army & Navy Register* 41 (Jan 5, 1907): 10.

36. *Army & Navy Register* 41 (Jun 29, 1907): 6; ibid. (Jul 13, 1907): 5. See also Rear Admiral Willard H. Brownson (ChBuNav) to Rear Admiral Robley D. Evans (CinC Atlantic Fleet), Jun 11, 1907, Brownson Papers, NHF, LC. The ships involved were *Iowa* and *Indiana,* which were placed "in ordinary" in order to man *Vermont* and *Kansas.*

37. Swinburne to SecNav, Sep 3, 1907, NA, RG 45:395/133 Pacific Fleet Letter Book, Aug 31, 1907–Jan 5, 1908 (Letters to Secretary of the Navy).

38. Unidentified enlisted man's letter, USS *Louisiana,* Nov 13, 1906, enclosed in E. McBeth to Theodore Roosevelt, Jan 16, 1907, NA, RG 24:88/1159–115.

39. "One of Dewey's Men," "The Blue Jacket's Point of View," *Army & Navy Journal* 39 (Mar 29, 1902): 757.

CONTRIBUTORS

DR. GRAHAM A. COSMAS is a historian with the U.S. Army Center of Military History and has authored or coauthored several books on modern American military history, including *An Army for Empire: The United States Army in the Spanish-American War, 1898–1899.*

REAR ADMIRAL MIGUEL A. FERNANDEZ, SPANISH NAVY, during 1998 served as Head of the Spanish Military Mission to the Supreme Allied Commander, Atlantic, based in Norfolk, Virginia. He is a graduate of the Spanish Naval War College.

DR. JOHN A. GABLE, Executive Director of the Theodore Roosevelt Association since 1974, is also the founder and editor of *The Theodore Roosevelt Association Journal.* He has published numerous scholarly works on Theodore Roosevelt and his impact on American life.

DR. JOHN B. HATTENDORF, the Ernest J. King Professor of Maritime History at the U.S. Naval War College since 1984 and Director of the Munson Institute of American Maritime History at Mystic Seaport in Connecticut since 1996, has authored, coauthored, or edited 30 books in the field of naval and maritime history.

LIEUTENANT COMMANDER HENRY J. HENDRIX II, USN, a veteran of the Persian Gulf War, has served in several naval aviation commands of the U.S. Navy since 1988. In 1994 he was awarded the prestigious Samuel Eliot Morison Scholarship in U.S. Naval History.

DR. EDWARD J. MAROLDA is Senior Historian of the Naval Historical Center in Washington, D.C. He has authored, coauthored, and edited a number of books on the history of the U.S. Navy, including *FDR and the U.S. Navy* and *Shield and Sword: The United States Navy and the Persian Gulf War,* which received the New York Council of the Navy League's Theodore and Franklin D. Roosevelt Naval History Prize.

DR. ANNA K. NELSON, Distinguished Adjunct Historian in Residence at American University, has published numerous books and other scholarly works on the history of modern American diplomacy and intelligence.

DR. JAMES R. RECKNER, founder and Director of the Vietnam Center at Texas Tech University, is a U.S. Navy veteran of the Vietnam War and author of *Teddy Roosevelt's Great White Fleet,* for which he was awarded the New York Council of the Navy League's Theodore and Franklin D. Roosevelt Naval History Prize.

DR. JACK SHULIMSON served as a supervisory and staff historian of the History and Museums Division, Headquarters, U.S. Marine Corps, from 1964 to 1999, and during that time he published numerous works on the nineteenth- and twentieth-century history of the U.S. Marine Corps.

DANA WEGNER, Curator of Ship Models for the Department of the Navy since 1980, has authored *Fouled Anchors: The "Constellation" Question Answered* and numerous scholarly articles on the authenticity of ships and events important to U.S. naval history.

INDEX